M000074884

GET ROOTED!

GET ROOTED!

Growing People and Companies Through Change

STACY HENRY

LIONCREST
PUBLISHING

COPYRIGHT © 2020 STACY HENRY

All rights reserved.

GET ROOTED!

Growing People and Companies Through Change

ISBN   978-1-5445-1585-4   *Hardcover*

        978-1-5445-1584-7   *Paperback*

        978-1-5445-1583-0   *Ebook*

To my cousin, Craig. Despite leaving this world too soon, your deep roots will always remind me why growing through change matters.

CONTENTS

INTRODUCTION

"Life belongs to the living, and he who lives must be prepared for changes."

—Johann Wolfgang von Goethe

The only constant in this world is change—a lesson I learned early on in life at the age of six.

It was a beautiful sunny day in the tiny little town of Leesburg where we lived. I was playing in our big beautiful house with my younger sister and our little brother, who was maybe three at the time, when we heard our mom call for us.

"Get in the car. It's time to go."

My mom corralled us into our gold-colored Pontiac hatchback— the nicest car we ever had. I don't remember much about that day. I don't remember packing. I don't remember what my sister, my brother, and I were doing when my mom gave the marching order. I don't even really remember getting into the car. But what I do remember has stuck with me. I remember my dad sitting on the big, wrap-around porch with his head in his hands, looking sad and defeated.

I looked at the shiny new car and compared it to my dad as he sat on that porch, our giant gray house rising up behind him. I remember thinking how dull he looked in comparison—and how very sad.

As I sat in the front seat looking back, I heard my little brother and sister ask, "Where are we going?"

"Things are changing," my mother said. "Things aren't going to be the same, but you're just going to have to deal with it."

And with that, we drove away. I didn't really understand the situation—what six-year-old could? I just remember looking out the window and feeling sad as I saw my dad watch us leave. Even as a six-year-old, I felt sorry for him. The thing that hurt my heart most was to see other people suffering.

Although I was a child and didn't understand what was happening, my gut told me it was a significant moment of change. I'm not sure why my mother chose that day to leave my father, but it led to their divorce and a whole new way of life for our family.

After that day, change followed me everywhere. Our home constantly changed as we moved from apartment to rental house, to trailer park, to my mom's fiancé's house, to the projects. Change flowed through the people who came in and out of our lives, and it flowed through the jobs that both my mother and my father had and then lost. Change continued to follow me throughout my childhood and stood beside me as an adult.

Change was the only thing that I could rely on—like a heads-down penny that kept showing up in my life. Now, if you aren't the superstitious type, let me explain that there is no luck granted with a heads-down penny. In fact, it's quite the opposite. This is definitely NOT a penny you want to pick up—only I figuratively did. Throughout every challenge and hurdle, I grew that heads-down penny into an entire trust fund. I learned how to handle change in ways that propelled me forward, not set me back. Through my various personal and professional experiences, I developed the tools necessary to face change with ease and confidence, and in this book, I'm going to show you how you can, too.

Don't you worry—this isn't a sad story about a broken kid or a "rainbows and butterflies" saga about how change is lovely. This is a story of change; however, the outcome is determined entirely by you.

CHANGE EQUALS GROWTH

Let's be honest, you're likely reading this book because you're facing change in your life—or with your company—and you're questioning what to do about it—and that's okay. Many people believe we simply *go* through change, but the greatest successes, both personally and professionally, come when we *grow* through change. We often view change as something bad that's happening to us, but we shouldn't look at it that way. Change isn't always bad; though many times it's hard and hard is sometimes painful. It's the hard and painful part of change that leads us to believe change is a bad thing. In reality, the pain we experience through change is actually growing pains. Change means growth—and growth is a good thing.

Growth, therefore, is what every company and individual should strive for, especially during difficult transitions—but how? You may ask yourself: How do I handle all these changes? How do I know I'm making the right choice?

While the answer isn't a simple one, it begins by taking responsibility for your own choices. Change is constant in all of our lives, and what it really boils down to is choice. You are in charge of how you handle change. We often make choices based on what feels comfortable right now instead of making choices that will benefit our future selves. We make choices that are driven by our limited experiences and motivated by our own biases. Many times, we don't even know how to make a different choice. This is because our decisions are made based on what we're rooted in—meaning they're based on what our core values are.

Your success in weathering through change is dependent on these values. What values are you rooted in? What are your company's values? For example, roots of dishonesty, selfishness, and control will lead to a downward spiral of the same dishonesty, selfishness, and control in those around you. Conversely, roots of integrity, service, and trust will result in an upward spiral of growth, which will lead to a more fulfilling life. The success of every company is dependent on its people and the values they're rooted in. Why? Because these values naturally influence us when we make our decisions. With a strong root system, we will naturally make better choices. And when we make better choices, we can stand strong and weather the inevitable winds of change.

GETTING ROOTED

In this book, I identify eight universal values to root ourselves in to help us grow and thrive, both personally and through corporate change. They are **love, relationship, trust, integrity, service, joy, spirituality,** and **progress**. Not only have these eight core roots been an important part of my life, they've also been a vital part of the companies I've both worked for and consulted with that have successfully grown through change. On the flip side, I also have experience with companies that were not rooted in these values, and things rarely turned out well for those companies. Some even had to close up shop and shut their doors for good. These universal values are key to successfully grow through change.

By the end of this book, I hope to do the following:

- Help you identify and evaluate your root system to see if it's working for you—and if not, to align you with what you want in life.
- Help you determine if you need to prune your roots, or move to more fertile ground.
- Help you embrace and grow the root system you already have to achieve bigger blooms. Not everyone needs a major overhaul. Maybe you just need some extra tools to help nurture and grow what's already there.

I will also explain the default root that grows if your core root isn't properly nurtured.

If you're a leader in a company, what you're rooted in matters. This book will help you understand the fundamental values that both you and your company must be rooted in to grow your company through a corporate change. I will also teach you and your team members how to incorporate these core roots personally, to strengthen one another and ensure everyone has the tools to not only grow through change, but approach it in a positive way.

If you're an individual looking for help to navigate the change in your life, this book will help you identify your root system and give you the tools to root yourself in core values. These fundamental tools will enable you to successfully grow through change. You may not always get to choose your circumstances, but you do get to choose how to face them. Growth comes by choosing to nurture these roots; make them a part of your everyday life.

It's my firm belief that one of the greatest tools to help us grow through change is self-reflection. Through self-reflection, we can not only determine what we're rooted in, but we can understand the "why" behind our actions. As such, you will find one hundred activities throughout this book to help you reflect on your life, your choices, and your motivations. Many of these activities are designed to discover what roots you lead with and what roots you need to get rid of. These activities will also help nurture your good roots. The more you practice, the more you'll strengthen your ability to weather life's storms.

A CAREER OF CHANGE

My root system grew out of the experiences I've had in my life. Through each experience, I have gained wisdom from those growing pains. I've also gained gratitude.

My ability to grow through change over the years became one of my greatest strengths. It has also allowed me to help others navigate their own change. In my career, this translates to training and coaching others on how to grow through corporate change and, especially, how to grow through personal change so that it doesn't affect the workplace. These skills have been invaluable to the companies I've worked for, and the teams I've both led and trained.

The crux of my career for well over two decades has been helping companies and their people move through change. Since the late 1990s, organizations like Iron Mountain, Bridgestone, and United Technologies have recruited me to help them think differently about what they were doing in the leadership space, and to help them create change to improve their organization. Even companies that I chose not to be a part of, like The Wonderful Company, XPO, and Boeing, have sought me for my expertise.

I've trained leaders to successfully manage their teams through change and helped companies change and consolidate their leadership development and talent management structures. My current role is at Collins Aerospace, a Raytheon Technologies Company. Collins Aerospace is one of the world's largest suppliers of aerospace and defense products and services. Over the course of eighteen months, I helped my C-suite leaders manage their teams through the largest change integration in the history of the company. We successfully brought two independent aerospace and defense companies—Rockwell Collins and United Technologies Aerospace—together into a single entity, Collins Aerospace.

Shortly after this integration, and just as we were getting ready to switch to autopilot, the entire world was thrown into massive disruption thanks to COVID-19. During this worldwide pandemic, while most of the nation worked from home, I supported top Collins executives, from an HR perspective, through yet another change. It was during this time that an aerospace and defense mega-merger happened—a merger between two behemoths: United Technologies and Raytheon.

I supported our chief financial officer, our chief communications officer, and our head of strategic development through the HR actions they needed to complete for this $75 BILLION merger of equals. I'm now leading these same execs through our "people actions," which include furloughs, synergies, and reductions in force—all part of the change we are currently faced with. If there's one thing I know, it's how to manage corporate change and the challenges that come along with it—even in the middle of a worldwide pandemic.

Over the past decade, I've helped people and companies think through their choices and encouraged them to get comfortable seeing things in different ways. When we open our eyes and minds to different approaches, we stop resisting change and learn to lean into it. That's when real growth happens.

While it's true that change is all around us, the ability to manage that change has always been an inside job.

WE HAVE WORK TO DO

Whether you're reading this book for yourself, or you're reading it to move your company through corporate change, putting in the work is the hardest part. I know you probably want a magic pill for this, but there isn't one. You have to put in the work if you want to see the growth. Change is going to come to each of us. The difference between those who rise and those who fall comes down to the choices you make and the work you do when faced with that change. If you read this book and apply its principles, not only will you strengthen your own resolve to face change courageously, but you'll learn how to strengthen others as well. You'll become a better person, a more successful leader, and you'll develop the resilience necessary to navigate every challenge you're faced with.

Going through change isn't easy. Making choices that are often uncomfortable isn't easy. It requires courage, hard work, and a lot of self-reflection. The desire to do the work is essential in order to move through change. If you fail to do the necessary work and neglect making intentional choices in a time of change, instead of bold, positive action, you'll become reactionary. And rather than managing change, the change will manage you. Stop making choices based on pure emotion and circumstance. Take the steps to face change head-on and come out the conqueror.

If you're faced with change and you desire to move through it successfully, I'm here to help.

Let's get started.

CHAPTER 1

EMBRACING CHANGE VS. HOLDING ONTO THE PAST

"In any given moment we have two options: to step forward into growth or step back into safety."

—ABRAHAM MASLOW

COVID-19

Repeat this unusual word to anyone, and not only do they know exactly what it means, but they're likely to have an emotional gut reaction to it. Like a frying pan in an old *Tom and Jerry* cartoon, the fallout from this simple unassuming word has smacked us alongside our heads and left our world spinning. No one asked for it, nobody even expected it, but we'll be dealing with the aftermath of it well into the next decade. The entire world has been thrown into a tizzy, and we're all figuring it out together.

Change happens to everyone, but not generally on such a grand scale, and very rarely all at once. Yet here we are together, experiencing one of the greatest changes in this generation's history. It doesn't take a scholar to recognize that because of COVID-19, things will never be the same. I get emotional when I think about it. It's literally changed the world, how we approach things, how we live from day-to-day, and how we approach each other. It's like World War II or The Great Depression, where every country in the nation is somehow affected by it. It's such a major point in history that it will forever be in the history books and will change the way we move forward.

Before COVID-19, the majority of us had our normal, day-to-day routines. Many of us unassumingly thought that because things had always gone a certain way, that life would always stay relatively the same. For years, and maybe even decades, this may have been our way of thinking. And why would we think any differently? We all have our own sense of normal, and that's what keeps us sane. It's like we subconsciously put ourselves in a glass house that obscures our view and keeps us from seeing the chaos around us. In our little glass house, we sanely sip our lattes and pleasantly peruse our social media feeds, unaware that change is coming. Then someone or something throws a rock through that glass house—like COVID-19—and the chaos pours in. Under these overwhelming conditions, people react in very different ways.

Some people fear change and hide from it. Others resist change and fight against it. But the people who embrace change and learn from it are those who will have the ability to grow through change and come out better on the other side.

We've all experienced change in life—maybe not a pandemic of epic proportions kind of change—but change, nevertheless. It's an inevitable part of our life. And if we want to grow and move as a people or a society, or even a world, we have to accept the change that comes. Otherwise, we remain stuck without any ability to move forward.

YOUR POWER TO CHOOSE

No one chose COVID-19. It came upon us quickly, like so many other inconvenient and demanding moments before it. And like all the other unannounced and unwanted moments of change, it forced us to think and act differently, possibly for the rest of our lives.

Because many times change is forced upon us, some may say that they don't have a choice in their circumstances. Some may even play victim to whatever happens in their life because of it. But even though we may not have the luxury of choosing our circumstances, we do, in all actuality, have a choice. We each get to choose how we move through change, grow from it, and show up on the other side of it—that will always be our choice.

Our choice is to act rather than react to the circumstances that surround us. During the COVID lockdown, many played the victim, sitting at home bemoaning life, blaming leaders of companies and countries, numbing their mind with television, food, or alcohol, all as the world continued to spin around them. While others chose to take actions to improve themselves. They knew they couldn't control their circumstances, but they chose to make a conscious choice to do what they could.

For some, those actions were directed inward with thoughtful contemplation and meditative practices to improve their mind and promote positivity. For others, their actions were more outward focused. They exercised more, learned a language, read good books, made improvements on their home, learned a hobby, and spent time connecting with family and friends. Some of us even wrote a book. All with that same world spinning around each of us. Those who made conscious actions to better themselves came out better on the other side of the lockdown.

When change happens to us, there are two paths we can take. We can resist the change by holding onto the past, or we can embrace the change by looking to the future. Both these choices have consequences, but only one allows us to grow and come out the other side a better person than we were going in.

When people choose to hold onto the past, they hold so tightly to what they know that they can't let go of the way things used to be. It's often a real struggle for many to imagine life any other way. When we're trying desperately to hold onto the past, we experience a major internal struggle wanting things to stay the same, or trying to force them back to the way they once were. This can create an inner turmoil that spills out everywhere. When we choose this path, not only does it cause serious anxiety in our own life, but it causes stress and strife for everyone else around us. When we choose to hold onto the past, it's like making a choice to superglue that glass house back together again with thousands of shards of glass. It's impossible to do and painful to watch.

When we face the future, we're more willing to let go of things that are no longer working, and we face the future with a brighter hope of what's to come. The only way to move through such cataclysmic change presented by COVID-19 is to recognize that we can't live in the past—we have to face the future with hope. This is a choice. Let me clarify that by no means am I saying it's an easy choice or a choice that will be pain-free; however, it's the right choice. This mindset isn't just for change caused by worldwide pandemics. It's the same mindset we need to face even the little changes in life.

SHIFTING YOUR MINDSET

Whether you realize it or not, change brings with it a wide array of choices. You can act or react. You can hold onto the past, or you can face the future. You can resist the change or lean into it. But whatever choice you decide to make, your mind is the place of origin. It's the jumping-off point of every decision you've ever made—even those bad decisions that you don't want anyone to know about. Believe me when I say I've made some of those decisions myself.

We make those poor decisions because we're human and we're all here learning, through our experiences, how to do things. But sometimes our humanness gets in the way and keeps us stuck. As humans, we each have the tendency to focus on the negative things that happen to us. It's what some psychologists call a negativity bias. We're also creatures of habit, and it's our natural tendency to seek the path of least resistance. We want what's safe and what's familiar to us. If we find ourselves in a situation where we perceive our safety is being threatened or we're in unfamiliar territory, our mind will naturally fight back. We'll give in to that negativity bias and come up with all kinds of reasons why we need to stay where we are and why change is bad for us. When we do this, we limit our ability to progress and grow. Because we're afraid of change, we unwittingly limit our own ability to change for the better.

When you and I actually make the conscious decision to lean into change and move through it, this doesn't mean that we're not acknowledging the other side. What it means is that we're acknowledging all sides with the understanding that we have options. And when we recognize we have options and lean into change, we're choosing a path that will lead us to better opportunities and future growth. A change mindset is a growth mindset and a complete shift from our natural tendencies.

It's important to recognize that shifting your mindset isn't always an easy process. This is not the path of least resistance. It requires both time and effort. But that effort will pay off in the long run. Shifting your mindset is a matter of constantly checking yourself and making the same decision over and over again every step of the way.

For example, when I wake up in the morning on the wrong side of the bed (please note, I am not a morning person, so as you can imagine, this is a very real scenario), I can consciously choose to shift my mindset to one of gratitude instead. I can also choose to make the effort to lean into that decision in order to better influence the direction of my day. Fifteen minutes into my day, when someone sends me an email outlining some reason why HR sucks, I may immediately find myself reverting to my human tendency of negativity. I may want to respond to the email with something negative of my own. This is exactly opposite of the mindset I had chosen for the day.

When this situation happens, I have to bring my mindset back to one of gratitude and remember that I have a choice. When other situations happen throughout the day that pull me away from my conscious decision to choose gratitude, I have to continue to remind myself of the choice I made that morning. It requires effort on my part. I have to act in those moments rather than react to the emotions that come from them. I have to choose gratitude over and over again until I've created a new pathway for my thoughts to go, and gratitude becomes my new mindset.

Doing the work to shift your mindset from one of comfort to a mindset of growth is fundamental to your ability to successfully manage change. No matter how you look at it, change equals growth.

LET GO OF WHAT'S COMFORTABLE

In order to shift any mindset, you have to get comfortable with being uncomfortable. I've managed change for the majority of my life, and I've come to realize that most people choose to stay where they're at because it's comfortable. Choosing to change means choosing to do things differently, and that can be very uncomfortable for people. I once had a client say to me, "I'd rather dance with the devil that I know than the one I don't."

This comment made the hairs on the back of my neck stand up. We shouldn't be content dancing with the devil at all. If we see change as something that's even worse than the bad circumstances we already find ourselves in, we're never going to figuratively find a better dance partner. We're just going to repeat that terrible dance over and over again—for the rest of our miserable lives. Sadly, that's what keeps us stuck and unable to grow.

Let me be clear: life doesn't have to be miserable! We get to choose how we react to every single circumstance. I wanted to shake that client out of complacency and remind him that dancing with the devil is still a choice that he was making. By resisting change, he was resisting growth. By not choosing something new, he was choosing to stay the same—even though he wasn't happy where he was at. Choosing to do nothing is still a choice. And like every other choice we make, there will always be consequences that come from that choice. In letting go of what's comfortable, and making that choice to change, we actually recognize that change isn't bad—it's a catalyst for growth.

I also want to point out that making the conscious decision to do things differently and letting go of what's comfortable doesn't mean abandoning everything. Anchoring ourselves in both personal and universal values is what will give us the greatest capacity to conquer change. These values will give us something to hang onto when life is thrown into chaos. If individuals and organizations lean on these values, especially in times of change, growth will be a natural consequence.

EMBRACE A VALUES-DRIVEN LIFE

The term "Values-Driven Leadership" has been around for

many years. It's the idea that leaders lead from an abiding sense of purpose. They're committed to life-affirming values that drive and enable themselves, their employees, and their organization to positively contribute to the society in which they live. These values-driven leaders serve as positive and genuine examples. They encourage employees to engage in a values-driven life. Through their leadership, they help to identify and align values that give both individuals and companies a greater sense of purpose. These values become a critical foundation for both individuals and companies in a time of transition.

Choosing to live a values-based life will provide something to hold onto when change happens, regardless of who we are or what our circumstances may be. Those values will become a lifeline in the time of a storm. They will become the thread that holds us together when it feels like everything else is falling apart. They will become a sure anchor and a guiding light when change brings its inevitable storm.

This is true for both individuals and companies. Organizations that choose a values-driven mindset will have a greater ability to move their entire company through massive change. As organizations clearly articulate their values, it strengthens their company culture and guides every decision that they make.

When values become the bedrock of what we say and do, change becomes much easier to manage. Because of this, we have to know what we believe in, and we have to practice that belief every day of our life. What do you believe in? Do you believe in a greater good? Do you believe that there is purpose to everything that happens? Do you believe in yourself? Do you believe in your family? Do you believe in your company? You've got to believe in something in order to get through change.

Without a belief in something, you're actually choosing to become apathetic. You've allowed yourself to become numb to the world (which, by the way, is a choice) and you've shut down any opportunity to grow.

Having something to believe in and living a values-driven life provides the hope that there's something better on the horizon. It also provides the desire and motivation to embrace change. Believing in something—especially yourself—serves as a catalyst to move you from resisting change to embracing what is possible through change.

FACE CHANGE HEAD-ON

Once you know the values you believe in and practice living those values regularly, you'll be better prepared to face change head-on. I never want to say that practice makes perfect, but I will say that practice makes progress. And the more you practice living a values-driven life, the more progress you'll make, especially in those transitional periods of life. You'll have the ability to fight the natural fears that come when presented with change, and you'll find more peace when in transition.

Let me give you two examples from my own life. One is a personal example, and one is from my professional life. Personally, at the beginning of the year, I decided that I wanted to make some positive changes in my life, so I created a vision board. To be honest, I had always made fun of vision boards but decided that this year, I was going to see what all the hype was about. I found words I wanted to believe in, including self-care, self-love, and Jesus. I also determined the values I wanted to incorporate to help transition me into a better version of myself. I put the vision board on my bathroom mirror so that every time I go into the bathroom, it's right there, staring me in the face. I see the words and images on it every day and make a decision on what I'm going to focus on.

As a side note, I'm happy to report to all of you vision board junkies that my vision board has now become a permanent part of my life. When I don't look at my board, I feel as if something is missing. It has become a necessary part of my routine. I've been practicing those values every day for several months now. When COVID came, these values anchored me. I noticed that I had an easier time with the changes brought on by the pandemic than several people around me, including my friends and colleagues. I'm not saying it was a party, but it hasn't been hard, either. The values I've practiced have become the lifeline that has saved me.

Professionally, before COVID-19, my company began the long process of merging with Raytheon, as I explained in the introduction. Then, like a thief in the night, COVID hit. With this massive merger and COVID creating the perfect storm, we began having an inordinate amount of furloughs and layoffs. Many in the company were frustrated with all the changes happening all at once and this brought a lot of pushback.

To make things even more challenging, it was my responsibility to make many of the unwanted phone calls that would result in the recipient's job loss, all while experiencing devastating work loss myself. I was given a 10 percent pay cut and fifteen days furlough with the expectation that it would only be a few months before I received the same kind of unwanted call from my own boss.

But before this process ever even happened, I made the conscious decision to believe in the company. I believed that they were trying to protect jobs wherever possible, and I also believed that they were making the best decisions for the company to sustain long-term success. When these massive layoffs came, it would have been very easy for me to talk bad about the merger, the company, and their decisions. I didn't, because I'd already made the choice to believe in my company and the leaders who had the difficult job of making the hard decisions. The change became easier for me because I knew what I believed in and let those values naturally drive my decision-making and overall thought process.

Embracing a values-driven life gave me the courage to face change head-on and provided me something firm to hold onto. Not only was I able to move through the personal change that COVID created, but I was able to help move my company through change as well. This is what a values-driven life can do for you, too.

THE FUTURE IS BRIGHT

As the world watched the COVID-19 virus spread across the globe and quarantines were put in place, the media and politicians all gave their predictions. Some of them were doom and gloom, and others gave messages of hope. But no one could imagine the impact that would result from such an event. We all knew it was significant. We all braced ourselves, instinctively knowing that things were about to change, even though we didn't know what that would look like.

As we look to the future, both as a society and individuals, there are many questions. Even with all our charts and projections, we can never fully predict where the events of the future will take us. Like with all change, the future is covered in a thick veil of uncertainty. We might wish to see the end of this journey, but that is not how change works. All we can do is take the next steps into that unknown. What lies on the other side means nothing compared to the people we will become when we get there.

This book isn't about making predictions or making that path any easier. It's about giving you the tools to fight back the fears that stunt our progression and keep us from realizing the opportunities that will inevitably present themselves during those moments of transition. When our guts are twisted from the prospect of life-altering change, we can stand firm, rooted in values that are enduring. We can grow through the change, rather than shrink from the fear.

I don't see a bright future because of some misguided hope or blind denial of what I face. Change is hard and scary. However, I know a bright future lies ahead because I know how to face change and persevere. I know how to grow stronger and more firm in those values that matter, despite the storms that rage around me. It is that resolve that I wish to share with you, so you can weather the winds of change and come out of the storm stronger and more rooted than ever before, ready to greet the new day with a brilliant vision of what is to come. That is the promise of those who *get rooted*.

PUTTING IT INTO PRACTICE

1. Identify one thing that you've held onto from your past that is no longer serving you. Determine the reasons WHY you've held onto it and what's keeping you stuck. Write down and implement small action steps you can take that will help you to let go.

2. Write down three aspects of your personal or professional life that would change if you stop holding onto your answer from number one. Once you let go of what's holding you back, what will you replace it with? Pick something that will help you move forward.

3. Write down one small change you can embrace in your current situation, personally or professionally. Keep it with you and reread it daily until you have embraced the change.

4. Identify the biggest change you need to embrace, either personally or professionally. Write down five positive statements about embracing that change and then say them out loud for five days.

5. Answer this question: How has holding onto the past versus embracing change impacted your ability to move forward or progress in _____?

6. Think about one change you have embraced and take five minutes to write down all the ways you successfully embraced that change. It's important we're able to recognize and celebrate when we do embrace change.

7. Think about someone in your personal life or company that has chosen to hold onto the past and answer these questions: How is it to interact with this person? Do I have any of those same potentially frustrating tendencies? This question isn't about comparison. It's about learning more about yourself by evaluating the example of others.

8. Think about someone in your personal life or company that has chosen to embrace change and answer these questions: What's it like to interact with this person? Do I have any of those same, potentially motivating tendencies?

9. Think about someone you know who seems to embody "embracing change" and ask them for a few tips on how they do it.

10. Fast forward one year from now: How will you describe your biggest accomplishment as it relates to embracing change versus holding onto the past?

CHAPTER 2

YOUR CENTERBRANCH AND ROOT SYSTEM

"If you watch how nature deals with adversity, continually renewing itself, you can't help but learn."

—Bernie Siegel

I'm not a botanist by any stretch of the imagination. I did, however, take a science class or two—just like every other high school and college student looking for that blessed diploma. But it doesn't take a degree in plants to have a basic understanding of how they grow. Consider this Plants 101 for those of you who might have forgotten those basics. This may seem like it doesn't apply, but work with me. I promise if you pay attention through this lesson, it's going to make sense to you in the end. Understanding the growth of a tree is essential to understanding the unique framework I use to teach people and companies how to grow through change.

So, why did I choose a tree for my framework? Well, a tree is something that every person can recognize. Whether it's a palm tree, a ficus tree, an aspen tree, an oak tree, a pine tree, a cherry tree, or even a cactus—everyone can visualize a tree. Some trees are tall, while others are short. Some are thin while others are so thick, you can cut a hole in the trunk and drive a car through it. Some trees thrive in the desert, while others grow in a tropical rainforest. No matter the shape, size, or environment, every tree is uniquely different and beautiful.

Trees are relatable because people are the same. We're all different. I'm uniquely me, and you're uniquely you. But most of all, just like trees, all humans have two things in common: we all have a root system, and we all grow.

HEALTHY ROOTS

Healthy roots make a healthy tree. A tree's root system absorbs oxygen, water, and nutrients from the soil and then carries those nutrients up through the tree to the branches, leaves, and blooms. The nutrients and water these roots carry throughout the tree are vital to a tree's growth. Roots also store the energy created by the tree through photosynthesis and make it available to the tree when it's needed, especially in the time of stress.

Another essential role of roots is that they anchor the tree in place, allowing the tree to resist the forces of wind, running water, or mudflow. They determine the tree's alignment and fight off other trees for the limited amount of resources available. Often the roots of a tree can grow larger and wider underground than the canopy of the tree that is visible above. What this means is that in order to evaluate the health and long-term performance of a plant, it's all about the roots.

Likewise, in order to evaluate the health and long-term performance of a person or a company that is moving through change, it's all about their root system. Like plants, we often value a person or a company because of their top growth, while ignoring the source of it all. And just like plants, the growth of both people and companies come from their root system and what lies underneath.

FINDING YOUR CENTERBRANCH

In addition to its roots, every tree also has what I like to call a centerbranch. It's at the center of the trunk and runs from the roots to the branches. It's the very heart and core of the tree. The centerbranch is what keeps the tree strong. But the strength of a centerbranch is largely determined by what it's rooted in. When this centerbranch is rooted in good ground, the tree is strong and able to grow and weather any storm. But if the ground is rocky with little nutrients, there is little opportunity for growth.

If you're scratching your head asking yourself what in the world this has to do with change, let me explain. This analogy can be applied to people and companies. We each have a centerbranch that lies at the very heart of what we do. It guides us in our decisions and determines how we move forward in life. The strength of each centerbranch is largely determined by what we are personally rooted in. When our centerbranch is rooted in good things, we are strong and growth continues to happen, regardless of the circumstances we find ourselves in. But when we're rooted in the wrong things, our centerbranch becomes weak, our tree becomes barren, and we're unable to move through change, no matter how hard we try to force it.

In order to demonstrate this, consider your life's mission statement, or the mission statement of your company. This is symbolic of your centerbranch. If your core driving mission is to "Be the good in the world," then in order to fulfill your mission, you would need to be rooted in values such as service, love, and relationships. The things you're rooted in will determine how successful you are in accomplishing your mission.

Sometimes there is a misalignment between a person's centerbranch and what they are rooted in. People may say their centerbranch is one thing, however they're rooted in values that don't align. For example, if someone said their centerbranch was faith, but they were rooted in greed and conflict, then growth wouldn't happen because those values do not align.

Misalignment between centerbranch and roots is often unintentional. More often than not, people don't realize they're rooted in the wrong things until they do the work to uncover it, or someone points it out to them. Other people may see it, but it's often a complete blind spot for us to see for ourselves.

For the longest time, I believed my centerbranch was love. My actual roots, however, were skepticism and blame, which contributed to my rocky marriage. It wasn't until much later that I realized there was a misalignment there. My decisions towards my husband weren't based on love, they were based on skepticism and blame instead because those made up my root system.

Our decisions replicate the values that we're rooted in, and growth can only come when our centerbranch and roots are aligned. Remember, it's the roots of a tree that determine its alignment. This is equally true with both people and companies.

As a company, if you told your team that your centerbranch was "One Team," but you were rooted in selfishness and control, your decisions would be determined by how you could control the situation and how you could get the most out of it. People would see that what you say and what you do are different from one another and your team would lose trust in you.

When your roots aren't aligned with your core, whether you like it or not, it will always come out in your actions.

YOUR PERSONAL ROOT SYSTEM

It's vital to understand what your centerbranch is rooted in because it strongly plays into your decision making. Your root system is the driving force behind the unsaid things that show up in what you do and how you treat people. These are things we often don't talk about, but we know they are there. They're felt rather than spoken.

The values you're rooted in influence every decision you make. For example, if a company executive is rooted in relationships, they subconsciously make decisions that create stronger connections with others, helping them tackle any hurdles. If this person is rooted in skepticism, on the other hand, they won't have the ability to lead with trust, which is a vital element to leading people in general, especially through a transition. Likewise, if the executive is rooted in greed, they won't make decisions that are beneficial for their company or their employees.

Once you successfully identify your values, you're half-way there. Afterward, you can either nurture those values if they are a good representation of who you want to be, or you can pull them up by the roots and root yourself in different values.

In my earlier years, my centerbranch, the core of everything I did, was self-preservation. I was rooted in things like fear, control, mitigating risks, and skepticism. Some of this was because of how I grew up, and some of this was simply because of who I am as a person. As a child, I assumed the role of "boss" for my sister and brother because I was the oldest. I was the one who took care of my siblings when my mom was at work. Every time she left, she legitimately said, "Stacy is the boss while I'm at work." My mother was always at work, so I was always the boss.

"Boss" was a badge I wore very proudly starting at age eight. I loved being the boss. I loved the authority over other people, albeit very little people. I loved that I decided everything from what clothes my sister and brother wore to what they ate to what they did. I would make the decisions on whether or not they had friends over or rode their bike to the park. I was really good at being the boss.

What I didn't know at the time was that this was the start of my control root. As time progressed and our family situation became more turbulent, the root of fear started to grow. There were actually two perspectives of fear—fear for our emotional and physical safety, and the unintentional fear that I would create in others if I didn't have a sense of control. These roots just continued to grow. Over time they began influencing my centerbranch, and ultimately my decisions, and I didn't even realize it.

As I entered adulthood and, ultimately, the workforce, those roots were still there. I would insert myself into situations and solve problems by trying to control every situation and the people around me. In 1999, I was hired as a manager for L.A. Weight Loss Systems in Pittsburgh. In full transparency, I thought I was being hired as a counselor since my degree was in social work (but that's another story for another book).

My job was to run the center while managing all consultations, aka *sales*. The entire staff was expected to sell weight loss programs and products to prospective clients at an 80 percent close rate. These were not small-dollar sales—a typical sale could range anywhere from $1,200 to $5,000 dollars.

I learned the art of the emotional sale very quickly and had a really high close rate. At that same time, I had employees who were not closing sales—at all. Instead of coaching or training them, I jumped in and took almost every sale. I took complete control of the store, took every consult, closed every sale, and thought my staff would be happy because I brought us to the number one store in our region, week after week. I really didn't trust them to do anything. Although I never said that, they felt it. Eventually, people quit, and I was left overworked and frustrated. In retrospect, I should have been frustrated with myself.

These corrupt roots led to more chaos and further corruption— more fear, more control, less trust, and more frustration—not just in my professional life, but also in my personal life. I thought my desire to "problem-solve" for people was coming from a root of helping others. It was most certainly not.

Let me clarify—when I say "problem-solve," what I really mean is that my way of helping was "telling other people what to do." This was ultimately me trying to control situations and outcomes driven from one of many roots like control, fear, lack of trust, etc.

Imagine, if you will, a very real scenario from my actual life that serves as a perfect example of what I'm talking about. This exchange was between me and someone dear in my life who we'll call Diana:

Me: "How are things with Joe?"

Diana: "OMG, so good. I am so happy!"

Me: (insert root of skepticism here) "That's awesome! I'm glad you're happy! How's Joe's ex? Are they divorced yet?"

Diana: "Everything is fine, I guess."

Me: "Fine sounds like a problem." (Root of control starting to come up here) "You should definitely not move forward with anything, at all, until you have proof that things are moving." (Blatant root of control here—not even masked as another root.)

Diana: "I trust that he's doing what he says."

Me: "Hmmmm…"

Me one day later: "I wanted to help and protect you, so I went to the courthouse to pull paperwork and Joe has not even filed for divorce. He lied to you. You should not be with him. You need to take care of your boys and not bring this drama into your life."

Diana: (I cannot actually print what was said next).

Me one year later: "I don't understand why you're still not talking to me."

Diana ten years later: Happily married to Joe with a young son.

While I'm making light of a very real and very painful personal scenario, it was ultimately my roots of skepticism, control, and fear for Diana and her sons' well-being that led me to make choices that really hurt our relationship. Because of these deep-seated roots, my life continued to move in a direction that I didn't particularly like, and I became a person I didn't even recognize.

Because of this, I did a lot of self-work. I dug deep and asked myself how I wanted to show up in the world. It certainly wasn't how I had been showing up. I knew I had to make a change.

In searching, I found my faith, which became my new center-branch. I wanted people to look at me and see my faith brightly displayed through my light. I wanted them to remember the hope in my smile and the kindness I showed them. In order to do this, I had to unplant myself from where I was, uproot the fear, control, and skepticism, and replace them with roots of integrity and service.

Unplanting my roots meant that I had to start trusting people. I had to actually show genuine love and kindness towards them. Every time skepticism began rearing its ugly head, I had to recognize it and make a different choice by nurturing the root I wanted to replace it with instead. It wasn't easy, and it was definitely a process. It required a great deal of self-reflection and self-awareness. However, by choosing to do the necessary work to unplant the roots that were causing me to remain stagnant, I was able to align my roots to a new centerbranch that has allowed me to continue to grow through many years of change.

My centerbranch of faith is now the core of who I am. That experience is a whole other book in and of itself. But the values I've rooted myself in because of it completely influence how I interact with those around me. It's how I show up in the world.

DETERMINING YOUR ROOTS

Sometimes it's hard to determine what your roots are, but they will show up in how you treat people. They will be felt in the actions that you take and the words that you speak. This is how you can also determine the roots of others. Most people don't go around spouting their beliefs or the values that determine and drive their decisions, but those things will always be felt by those around them.

You can determine the roots of a person by examining the fruits that come from their figurative tree. If the roots are good, it will be good fruit. Examples of good fruits in leaders are wisdom, understanding, patience, counsel (or coaching), a strong team, and a legacy for developing talent. My current leader is known for the talent that comes out of her organization. She has always been able to identify, coach, and develop early career talent into strong leaders. Over the years, she created a substantial pipeline of leaders, many of whom are top executives in the organization. She is rooted in service to others and this produces the fruits of wisdom, counsel, and patience—all values she shares with others to grow great leaders. Good roots mean good fruits.

Conversely, if people are rooted in the wrong things, there will be very little fruit, or the fruit will be rotten. Now I'm not saying that people are rotten, although if I'm being honest, I may have thought that about a colleague or two through the years. But many times, what a person does is rotten because their roots are rotten and rotten roots can't produce good fruit.

When words and actions don't align with each other, it will produce a negative environment. And that negative fruit will be felt by everyone. Similarly, when rooted in the wrong things, a person may appear strong for a time, but underneath, they're withering away. And over time, the weakness in their root system will certainly be revealed.

I've had a few leaders and know a few people rooted in the

wrong things, like greed, gossip, and envy. Their fruit—well, you know what they say about a bad apple…

I recently encountered, actually endured, someone like this. She was rooted in gossip and was missing the root of self-love. She had access to highly confidential information and would occasionally leak details to me couched as a "heads-up." At first, she would share information about people and situations that seemed helpful. However, I quickly realized she was sharing confidential information that I should not have access to. She would also gossip at length about many people we both worked with.

I finally asked her not to engage in gossip and told her she should not be sharing confidential information with me, regardless of whether or not I was in HR. The fruits that came from that tree afterward were quite bitter. I was subject to snide remarks, left out of important meetings, found it difficult to gain access to my executives' time, and ultimately she reported an unsubstantiated claim that I was misusing company time. After six weeks of investigation, the claims were found to be untrue.

When it was realized by many that her fruits were not exactly good, she eventually left the company and decided to replant somewhere else. As personally painful as that was, I don't think she was aware of what she was rooted in, or how to even change it. Having the ability to change roots that run deep requires a great deal of self-reflection while holding the mirror up to our face. It also requires the willingness to actually make a change.

To determine what we're personally rooted in, a great question to ask ourselves is: How am I showing up in the world, and what kind of fruit am I producing? For some of us, like my colleague, we may not even know the answer. Sometimes, how we perceive ourselves, versus how people around us experience us are really two different things because we don't really understand what we're rooted in.

One of the best ways around that is to simply ask others how we're showing up to them. How are people perceiving you, and does it align with how you want people to perceive you? If the two don't align, then you have some work to do. If you're not showing up in the best light for others, spend some time identifying how you want to show up. How do you want others to experience you? Our centerbranch is the part that people see. If you want people to see you as a kind, generous person, you need to make sure you nourish roots of service and relationship in order to support those values you want to represent.

As the leader of a company, a good place to start is your mission, vision, and value statements. Are they true? Are they accurate? Or are they just nice words written on a poster in your conference room? You may claim you believe them, but your employees will know by your actions what you really think. If your actions don't match what you say your values are, your employees will know it and it will create a negative energy in the workplace. For example, if a foundational principle of your company is trust and yet you micromanage everything an employee does, they won't trust you, and they'll know you don't trust them.

It's essential that your words and actions align with one another in order to navigate change successfully.

READJUSTING YOUR ROOTS

Ask yourself the question: *What values am I rooted in?* In actually determining the current values you're rooted in, it's important to be honest about it. Don't lie to yourself. This isn't just a fun, feel-good activity to boost your self-esteem. As a matter of fact, when you really get down to the roots of your decision making, you may not like what you find. But that's okay—actually, it's better than okay because this book is going to teach you how to fix the things that have kept you stuck. When you're real and honest with yourself about what motivates and drives you, you can change those things that are keeping you stuck and actually experience real growth.

After you've honestly evaluated your root system, and if you've determined it needs to be adjusted, you have an important choice to make. You can prune back your roots, replant them in better soil, or simply nourish the roots you already have.

PRUNING

Cutting off the dead parts or trimming back some of the branches that are taking a majority of the nutrients is an important part of the tree's continued growth. It's the same kind of idea when pruning your roots. And no, I'm not talking about cutting off a limb or two. I'm talking about making small self-adjustments to show up better than before.

If you know your centerbranch is "To create value in the world and make a difference," but you find yourself disengaged most of the time instead of rooted in people and relationships, you can make slight adjustments that will help you get to where you want to be. This may require you to shift a limiting thought process, change negative behaviors, switch-up a routine, or change the people you're hanging out with.

In an organization, there are many small adjustments you can make to prune your roots and better align them with your centerbranch. Minor adjustments may include changing your thought patterns, getting into a healthy routine, adjusting the company you keep, moving departments, or taking a stretch assignment. It could even be doing more service, especially as a company.

At Carrier, we were heavily involved with Habitat for Humanity. Full teams went to do house builds on a quarterly basis. We would spend an entire day out of the office to give back to the community. Service allowed us to come together as a team and nurture our relationship root. It was simple to make the decision to give back to the community, but in giving back, we more fully aligned with each other.

By making small but significant adjustments to your life, you can essentially trim back those things that are taking the bulk of your energy and refocus that energy back into those roots that are the most important.

REPLANTING

Sometimes, pruning your roots isn't enough because no matter how much you cut off, good roots can't grow in bad soil. Some people may look at their current root system and recognize that small adjustments won't change a toxic environment. They may equally feel that their current root system needs a huge overhaul because they've remained stagnant for far too long.

And sometimes, in extreme cases, because of a person's current circumstances, or because of the state of the world around them, a person may realize that their root system has shifted and grown into something completely unrecognizable. When these realizations come, it may be time to move your entire tree to more fertile ground.

When I was in my twenties, I was having the time of my life. I was young, successful, and hungry for more. The people I surrounded myself with were, what I like to call, ego monster maniacs (I promise it's a real thing). And my root system became entangled with theirs. I went from being humble and grateful to greedy, entitled, and expectant. In other words, I became an ego monster maniac, too.

One day, I paused and took a good look at who I was, and I was shocked by my behavior. It was an incredibly painful moment for me. I sadly realized that the roots I had nourished were leading me to become a version of myself that I didn't even like or even recognize anymore. I realized in that moment that in order to align my root system to who I wanted to be, I had to stop engaging with those people who I had allowed myself to become entangled with. It was a painful process. It didn't feel good for them, and it didn't feel good for me. It was incredibly hard, but it was absolutely the right thing to do.

Sometimes, we may even find ourselves in difficult situations where we let our root system die altogether. We stop nurturing any roots and let go of everything we hold dear. When this happens, we've got to dig deep and find those values that will help us survive and thrive, and root ourselves in them. In order to weather and grow through change, we've got to have something to hold onto that will anchor us in the times of a storm. Because if we don't have something to anchor us, just like trees without any roots, the winds are sure to carry us away.

NOURISHING THE ROOTS YOU ALREADY HAVE

While pruning and replanting roots may require drastic changes, you may discover that your roots are good, but they don't yet run deep. This is a good thing. It means that you just need the necessary tools to help nurture and grow what you already have. This may seem super cheesy, but what you need is Miracle Grow. You've got the strong centerbranch for your tree and the right root structure—you just need those roots to grow deeper so you don't tip over when the storm comes.

You can begin by evaluating what is already working in your life. Where are you seeing growth? Find those areas and capitalize on them. How can you do more of those things that are providing you with your greatest growth and genuine happiness? For me, it was doing more service work, volunteering, and giving back. Once I started spending my time helping others, I grew in service, in connection through relationships, in joy, and in love. So many values can be nurtured through service to others. It was like Miracle Grow for my soul. And in nourishing and deepening my roots, I also strengthened my centerbranch of faith.

For some, nourishing your roots may mean getting a mentor. It could mean asking people what they see as your strength and working to improve yourself in that area. Sometimes, it may even mean having the confidence to move something forward that would otherwise scare you to death.

An example of that for me is writing this book. I've been saying for ten years that I wanted to write a book, but never actually had the confidence to move it forward. I was rooted in self-doubt, complacency, and a fear of failure. I did a lot of work to get rooted in the right things to finally make this book a reality. As my roots grew deeper, I began to nourish them more, and my confidence grew. The roots that held me back from writing my book were overtaken by the roots I intentionally nourished. When it's all said and done, I'll have a published book from start to finish in ten months! Ten months is nothing in comparison to the ten years I was stuck. Now, that doesn't mean it's been an easy ten months. It's been very difficult—but so worth it.

Nourishing your roots means making the conscious choice to accept a growth mindset—to seek it out, and to do the work to make it happen.

A WORD OF CAUTION

Change and transition is hard. It's uncomfortable. And we are creatures of comfort. Because of this, it's incredibly easy during times of transition and change to slip back into what feels comfortable. Even with the best of intentions, you may occasionally slip back into making decisions based on old tendencies. But when things get hard, uncomfortable, and even vulnerable, that means you're doing it right. You have to get comfortable with being uncomfortable. This will be a great driver for overall growth. The greatest change you will ever make is this change inside yourself.

GET ROOTED!

There are many values we can root ourselves in, but through my years of experience, I've discovered eight universal values that have had the biggest impact holistically on both individuals and companies. Some of the best leaders and people that I've worked with are rooted in these very values.

These eight values are love, relationship, trust, integrity, service, joy, spirituality, and progress. When rooted in these values, each value becomes an anchor in the time of a storm.

When individuals and companies are not rooted in these values, natural human tendencies tend to take over. This is especially true in heightened times of difficulty and change. In lieu of love, conflicts will arise. Instead of forming relationships and connections, there will be complete disengagement. Rather than trust, control will become the guiding factor. Without integrity, dishonesty will run rampant. Lack of service will breed selfishness. Without joy, feelings of complacency will arise. Lack of spirituality will lead to a void of what I call nothingness. And the need for perfection will trump a person or company's ability to progress.

Rather than defer to our negative natural tendencies, we can make the conscious decision to root ourselves in these eight positive universal values. This is what will enable us to successfully navigate through life's changes.

The next eight chapters discuss each value in detail. You can read through them in order, or turn to the value you need to work on the most. If you struggle with perfection, learn how to uproot that perfection and focus on progress instead. If your tendency is to control people or situations, turn to the chapter on trust and learn how to more fully trust yourself and others. In every chapter, there's information that will help you overcome the negative human tendency and nourish the positive value instead. You'll also discover why each value is important and how to make it work for you.

Change happens one person at a time. One person willing to make a change can then help other people see the vision, which leads to other people expanding their views. Then it spreads and it spreads and spreads in an incredible upward motion until an entire organization is on board. But you can't inspire change unless you're willing to first make the change yourself.

These eight values have changed my life and the lives of countless others. They can change your life, too—if you're willing to do the work.

PUTTING IT INTO PRACTICE

1. Name your top three most important roots.

2. Answer this question honestly: Are you rooted in the right things? If yes, why do you feel this way? If no, what do you need to be rooted in instead?

3. Identify one root that you may need to prune back, such as skepticism, selfishness, mistrust, etc. Write one action you can take to begin that process.

4. Identify one root that you want to strengthen, such as love, relationship, trust, etc. Write down one action that you can take to nourish this root.

5. Take five minutes in a quiet place and think about all the ways your current circumstances (personally and professionally) are strengthening or weakening your root system. Of everything you thought of, what are three actions you will take?

6. What is one change you can embrace to nourish your entire root system?

7. Identify and name what you think your centerbranch is. If you told people this, would they agree or disagree?

8. Draw a picture of a tree and a roots system. Label each of the roots and centerbranch for your *current* state. Then, cross off the roots and/or centerbranch you don't want and redraw your future/ideal state.

9. Do a gut check activity: Do your roots and your values match? Spoiler alert—they should. If they don't, you have work to do...start at the top.

10. Identify one person (personally or professionally) that you feel is rooted in the right things. Write down what you think they are rooted in. Have a brief conversation with this person and ask them about their roots. Pro-tip—you may want to use the word values instead of roots, unless you want to give them my book as a pre-read requisite for your conversation.

CHAPTER 3

LOVE VS. CONFLICT

"If you can't change it, change your attitude."

—Maya Angelou

I'm quite certain that you just read the title of this chapter and flinched a little. Be honest, you did, didn't you? You're probably thinking to yourself that love has no business being in the workplace. But I'm just going to tell you, right now, that you're wrong. I'm not even going to sugarcoat it. You need to make *love* a priority in your workplace.

I'm not talking about romantic love or a tryst in the workplace. Of course, that should be avoided. But in avoiding the very idea of love, organizations are missing a key root in a thriving root system. The kind of love I'm talking about in this chapter is the kind of benevolent love we should have for the people around us. It's about being well-meaning, respectful, and kind.

If you're still not of the opinion that there's no place for love in the workplace, let me ask you this: Is it important to listen carefully to your employees and coworkers and help them feel valued and respected? Is it appropriate to show genuine support and concern for someone who is experiencing a difficult challenge? Is it valuable to give kind words of encouragement and speak to your boss with mindful and thoughtful language? All of these things are perfect examples of love in the workplace.

I'm going to go out on a limb and say that most companies who are experiencing conflict in their workplace are struggling because they aren't allowing love to be an active part of their work experience. Why? Because conflict is what occurs when benevolent love is absent in an environment.

ACCEPT NEW CHALLENGES

When I left my job in Philadelphia to live in Chicago and work for Bridgestone Retail Operations (BSRO), I was stoked about the job. They had actively recruited me, so I knew that they really wanted me—and who doesn't want to be wanted? I had trepidation about leaving Iron Mountain because I loved my team and the company. However, this new adventure was to help BSRO build what they called "a world-class training organization," and I was up for the challenge. After all, change is my middle name.

I've found that when I face new challenges with a positive attitude, it makes a significant difference in my ability to succeed. It's the same strategy for all of us. Embracing new challenges with a positive attitude is one of the greatest formulas for growth.

At the time I was hired, the CEO was new as well and he was really honest with me. He confessed that one of BSRO's biggest pain points was their training organization. When I asked a few more questions, he shared that many of the current trainers were employees who had transitioned from roles like technicians, service associates, or store managers to become trainers. In other words, they were subject matter experts on the role that they had been in—they were not formally trained as educators. While many of these "trainers" were effective, they were still being used in the wrong capacity. They had the technical knowledge and subject matter expertise; however, they weren't content creators, instructional designers, or facilitators. Being a trainer is an actual profession, and the company needed trained educators to work with their technicians to create content that could move their company forward.

"It's literally a disaster," the CEO said. "If we want to build the best automotive retail brand in the country, we need to start thinking about the training function." He assured me that I would have a seat at the table, the autonomy, and the authority to "fix the disaster." It all sounded great to me!

Since this was what I accomplished at Iron Mountain, it was

an easy decision. Not only was it a bigger job, a better offer with more pay, and an opportunity to live in a new city, it also sounded super sexy and exciting to me. I loved the idea of creating a world-class training organization, having carte blanche, and a $20 million budget to do it.

When I started, the employee I was replacing had been with the company for forty-four years and was leading the training function for the last fourteen of those years. It became evident that he also wasn't actually ready to retire, which made things incredibly awkward since there was a two-month overlap for knowledge transfer. The company valued promoting from within but occasionally strayed from that from time to time. I happened to be one of those times. In fact, I was one of less than twenty people who had been hired externally for a corporate role in the company in a quarter of a century.

My ultimate responsibility was to consolidate seven training functions into one and to centralize it. I was up for that challenge, because I really believed in what I was doing, and the good I could do for the company. My boss at the time, along with the CEO, encouraged me to take the first three months and learn the business, to meet people, and to lay the groundwork of what he wanted me to accomplish.

LEARN TO MOVE IN UNEXPECTED DIRECTION

Shortly after I was hired, however, the CEO had a new vision for the company, which he was very excited about. He called it *Vision 2020*. It was a holistic approach to becoming the country's premier automotive retailer of choice and a premier place to work by 2020. As part of that vision, he let go of a significant number of tenured and beloved leaders. This included my boss. Talk about life throwing you a curveball! Although it was done in an effort to "revitalize" the leadership team with outside perspective, it felt like he didn't value the perspectives or the history of the employees who have been a part of the company for an extended period of time. The employee sentiments around Vision 2020 were not good. And when I say not good, what I really mean is that it was like shouting an F-bomb during Sunday mass.

One day, the CEO came into my office and stood directly in front of me, put both hands on my desk, leaned in like a giddy child, and said something to the effect of, "Oh, Stacy, I have the best news ever! We just hired your new boss!"

He then went on a diatribe about how we needed to infuse the company with diversity in all forms to get a fresh new perspective. He said he told the executive search firm that he wanted to bring in someone who would shake up the organization, someone who didn't look or act like a "tire store guy," someone who would help him achieve Vision 2020, and someone to show BSRO what good looked like. He ended the conversation by mentioning that the actual qualifications of the job were secondary and that tires weren't rocket science. Then, he turned around and nearly skipped out of my office. I felt like I was in the twilight zone.

While I emphatically agree that diversity is essential to any organization, I also emphatically declare that qualifications matter! My gut was telling me this was going to be bad. My inner voice said, "Run back to Iron Mountain." I wish I would have listened to my inner voice because what happened next is the stuff that work nightmares are made of.

My new boss was your typical alpha male—very bold, very dominant, and a very loud human being. Where my philosophy was honoring the past and not burning down villages, his philosophy was the opposite. He brought several people with him from his previous company, and they razed the village and burned it to the ground—with the people still in it.

The company was doing quite well for itself before it was burnt to the ground. However, this boss and his little posse came onto the scene and made people feel like everything they had done was wrong. Their operations were wrong, their training was wrong, and the people were wrong. It's as if they came in with a flame thrower and annihilated everyone. And anyone who disagreed with their way of doing things was let go.

He mandated that everyone implement all of the same procedures that they had at a big-box retail store in an automotive world, which didn't work. And when it didn't work, he blamed everyone else. The only people he didn't blame are those people who he brought with him. They were all promoted.

WAR IS NOT THE ANSWER

I didn't agree with that philosophy, so I started voicing my opinion. Since I'm also a very strong, dominant individual, my new boss and I were like oil and water. The minute he realized he wasn't able to control me, the conflict started.

Conflict is actually an understatement. There was an all-out war between us and there were casualties on both sides. Neither one of us handled the situation well. Not only were we hurting ourselves, we were hurting the people around us. We created a very negative environment.

The following eight months were sheer terror for me. Everything I did, he undid. Every time I had a conversation or moved something forward in terms of store manager training or technician training, he came right behind me and said, "Nope, that's not what we're doing. We're undoing that protocol."

At one point, he asked me to plagiarize training material from his prior company. When I said no, I sat through a two-hour meeting where he shared his disdain for me. Over the course of those two hours, he shared all the reasons I sucked at my job. He undermined me publicly in executive meetings. Every time I started a sentence, he would interrupt me, and even went so far as to tell me in front of all my peers in a meeting that I was the worst training professional he had ever worked with.

His exact words, still burned into my ears, were: "I want you all to look at Stacy—she is an example of a failed leader. Don't be like Stacy."

I just have to point out that the year prior to this, I won the CUBIC ® Global Learning Leader of the Year award. Not only that, I have received numerous Corporate University Best-in-Class awards and had many case studies published in *Training Magazine*, Corporate Learning Network, Corporate University, ATD, *Chief Learning Officer* magazine, and *Workforce Management* magazine. I knew that I was good at my job, and there was a great deal of evidence that others knew it too. Even still, this boss told everyone that he was going to make an example out of me because I was what failed leadership looked like.

He may have made me cry a little in that meeting. For the record, I don't cry when I'm sad, I cry when I'm mad. And when I'm mad, you can be certain conflict follows.

We just had conflict at every turn. I struggled to see the good in him, and he obviously couldn't see any good in me. The more he pushed me, the more he created purposeful conflict with me. And the more conflict there was between us, the more I saw anything but love and respect for him. Benevolent love and genuine kindness wasn't even a blip on the radar. Everyone suffered because tensions were high. The workplace became a volatile space, and everyone was uncomfortable because of it.

YOU AIN'T GOT NOTHING IF YOU AIN'T GOT LOVE

In the middle of this very heated conflict, I blamed everything on my new boss. I saw everything as his fault. In retrospect, I recognize that the more he mistreated me, the more disrespectful I was to him. The default for both of us was conflict. I often wonder if things would have turned out differently if I had made the conscious decision to show up as my best self.

Since this experience, I've made the conscious decision to choose to live in a place of love. In situations of conflict, I choose to be kind, and this has made all the difference.

Love really does make the world go round. Because of this, love is the critical component to everything we do. It should be the main root in your root system and the launching point of every other value that follows. If you don't have a sincere love for people, then relationships, trust, integrity, service, and every other value will be affected.

Without love, our centerbranch cannot grow. Instead, our tree remains stagnant and hollow, and conflict naturally fills the void. Where there's no love, conflict is our default. And if conflict is our default, change can't happen. This is why love is an essential value to root ourselves in. The love and respect we have for each other as human beings and fellow travelers in this life is a vital part of both our personal and professional lives.

If a leader who is guiding people through change chooses conflict over love, one of two outcomes will happen: fight or flight. Either people push back and fight that leader tooth and nail, creating additional conflict. Or that leader will cause people to retreat and fall in line, discouraging both innovation and creativity. It's never a good situation when people are afraid of conflict and choose not to introduce new ideas that are contrary to the leader's view. When this happens, employees become stifled and companies fail to grow.

As a leader, love should be your rally cry. You can't do anything without it. When you choose love as your rally cry, you'll have the ability to move entire companies through incredible change and come out the other side better. And when your rally cry is loud enough, not only will you move people in a positive direction, you'll create lasting echoes that will move much more than just the people around you. Without love, you can't move people in the right direction and you'll often lose the good people that you already have.

LOVING ISN'T ALWAYS EASY

Love is a root that constantly needs work and nourishment. Choosing to be rooted in love means choosing to see people from a lens of kindness and mutual respect. It's giving them the benefit of the doubt and withholding biased judgments. It's choosing to see a person's good qualities and magnifying them, instead of accentuating the bad.

As human beings, our ability to love someone is much easier if we make it a conscious choice to approach every relationship through the eyes of love. When we're rooted in love, it will become the value we use to see the world.

Through my own experience, I've learned that it's much easier to make the decision to love someone before we meet them, rather than when we're in conflict. It's incredibly difficult to choose love and see the good in people when we're in disagreement.

When I was in conflict with my new boss, I couldn't see any good in him. In retrospect, I know he wasn't a horrible human being. I'm sure he was a good family man and had some good qualities outside my experience with him. I just couldn't see them. My view was limited by how he treated me. And eventually, I just stopped trying to find the good in him. I became numb to the situation, to the conflict, and to him.

Conflict is painful. When we're in conflict, the pain is real and that fight-or-flight mode becomes our only way of dealing with the situation. Instead of acting rationally, we become reactionary, and our emotions become our decision-maker.

That doesn't mean we have to remain stuck in conflict. There's always a way out. It won't be easy, yet it's very much possible as we learn to change our mindset.

The first thing we can do when in a situation of conflict is recognize that we have a choice. We can make a purposeful decision to choose love over conflict before we confront a difficult person. We can take a deep breath, count to ten, and stop letting our emotions make our decisions for us. And if we struggle to find the good in someone, we can make an honest effort to catch them doing something good, and then keep a journal of those good deeds to remind us of their good qualities. We can write them a thank-you note or give them a compliment. Most importantly, we can let the fruit of our actions become good, and see if it changes the fruit of theirs.

If we've done all we can, and our positive efforts aren't working, sometimes the only thing we can do is walk away. This is what happened with me with my new boss. When I realized I was becoming numb to even myself, I had to make a choice. Do I continue living in an environment of conflict, or do I walk away? Part of me wanted to stay just out of spite. Despite everything, I was successful. I centralized the company's training function and everybody was really happy with the change. I could have stayed where I was at, forcing myself to adapt and find success, but instead, I chose to make a change.

I transferred to a different area in our corporate headquarters and took myself out of the situation altogether. Some people viewed my resignation as me failing; I viewed it as me succeeding. This is because I was true to myself. I refused to allow the conflict to overcome and change me. I had a choice, and I chose me.

THE IMPORTANCE OF LOVING YOURSELF

Love isn't just a value for the workplace. It's an essential value for every aspect of our lives. This is especially true when it comes to loving ourselves. When it comes to our ability to love others, we can only love them at the capacity that we love ourselves. If we have a negative judgment or bias against ourselves, we are going to see that same judgment carry over to others. This is why when we're rooted in conflict, it becomes a real struggle to love anyone, including ourselves.

When I was in constant conflict with my boss, I didn't love myself and acted like a different person. Because my boss was critical of me, I grew more critical of the work that others were doing. I found myself even micromanaging because the one thing I could control was the quality of work from my team. As things spiraled out of control, I became incredibly judgmental of the work that my team was doing. I wasn't a peach to work with; it was a far cry from who I once was.

During this time, I was in a constant state of emotional, mental, and physical exhaustion. I wasn't healthy, and I started to show up that way. I would also show up as negative and disgruntled—and it wasn't just at work. People in my personal life started to notice as well, and they would confront me about it, which would, of course, lead to more conflict.

One day, I looked in the mirror and I realized I didn't even like myself. I asked myself how I was going to ever like the situation that I was currently in. And I realized that I never would. That's when I made the choice to change things.

In that moment, I realized that the only person I should ever expect love and kindness from is myself. I couldn't make other people's choices for them, but I could make better choices for me. I chose to do some much-needed self-care and went to counseling to talk through the conflict that had become a part of me. I made sure to navigate my emotional state, just as well as I did my physical state.

Making an effort to work through our own emotions and to take care of ourselves is an important part of growing through change. A tree can't grow if there are things eating at its roots, and neither can we. We have to recognize the source of the problem, make the effort to weed those problems out, and then regularly nourish our roots. This is how we'll grow.

LOVE REALLY IS THE ANSWER

It took a long time for me to overcome the experience I had

with that boss. I moved from Chicago to Nashville to take the job at Bridgestone America's headquarters, and it was a relief for me to get away from him. Yet there was still residue left. It was like that sticky residue that's left on the bottom of your shoe after you pull off a piece of gum that you've stepped on. We still had to go to functions where we would be forced to interact. It was painfully uncomfortable when we saw each other. I continued to have this distaste in my mouth for him. It certainly wasn't healthy. It didn't help that he kept trying to provoke me in every situation that he could. On the outside, I was tough and wouldn't allow it. I chose not to fight with him, which lessened his ability to fight with me. Nonetheless, there was still that inner conflict boiling up inside of me.

As I moved further and further away from it, I was able to reflect on that time. It wasn't a good situation for either of us. There's no question that I was mistreated, but I mistreated him too. When I stepped back and viewed him from a place of love and respect, I realized that he really had added value to the company. It's just a matter of how you looked at it, and what mindset you were in to see it there. Letting go of the conflict allowed me to see him as a person who was just trying to do his job. He just had a different perspective than mine.

This is what seeing people and situations through the eyes of love can do for us. Love helps us see things that we never knew were there. Love can teach us that there's good in every difficult situation. And love can even help us see the good in ourselves.

If I were to see that boss again today, it would be a respectful conversation. I wouldn't work for him again. Still, I can extend him the grace and respect that I would expect others to extend to me. And that's how it should be. Seeing him through the eyes of love allowed me to finally come to a place of peace and respect for him.

When facing change, rooting our centerbranch in love will give us the greatest chance of survival. It will help us to strengthen every other root system. Choosing to see the world through benevolent love and kindness is not just a mindset; it's a way of living. And it will help us to manage the change that shows up in every aspect of our life. The fruits of love are patience and forgiveness for others and for ourselves. This is why love should be the main root of our centerbranch and the very first root that we nurture and grow. When our love root is strong, every other root of our centerbranch is nurtured too.

PUTTING IT INTO PRACTICE

1. Identify one thing about yourself that you love. Write it down and nurture this quality for the next week.

2. Say (or think if you aren't at a point to say yet) three positive things in a meeting about someone you have conflict with. This must be sincere, or it will stink like a smelly fish on the table. It doesn't have to be grandiose. It could be as simple as, "He wears a pocket square well."

3. Think about your relationships at work and in your personal life. Are most of those relationships conflict-based or love-based? If they are conflict-based, write down three reasons that you might be creating conflict.

4. Handwrite a thank-you note to someone in your office or life acknowledging one thing that you appreciate about them. Maybe consider not signing it, or not telling the person it's from you. When we do things from a place of love, we shouldn't expect anything in return.

5. Next time you're in conflict, pause, count to ten, and ask yourself if the conflict is you. If so, make a choice to react differently.

6. Look at an area in your life where there's conflict. How would the conflict be different if you approached it with kindness? Keep a log of the opportunities you have to show love or change a thought pattern.

7. How is love showing up in your life, and are you nurturing this key root? Choose one way to nurture this root every day for a week. This could be as easy as choosing to genuinely smile at everyone you meet.

8. Create one affirmation you can say every day to be kind to yourself. Say it every day until you believe it and then create a new affirmation and repeat the process.

9. Take someone you're struggling with and find one thing you like about them that is positive (and if you're brave, tell them).

10. Make tick marks on your calendar of how many times you say something nice each day to the people around you.

CHAPTER 4

RELATIONSHIP VS. DISENGAGEMENT

"Coming together is a beginning, staying together is progress, and working together is success."

—HENRY FORD

If your plan is to live in a cave as a hermit for the rest of your life, you can disregard this chapter. However, as we learned from our most recent worldwide pandemic, social distancing and locking ourselves away from the world brings with it a whole new set of problems. Sitting in isolation, many of us came to the realization that we need each other. People are meant to connect, and not just through social media. No matter who you are or where you come from, nurturing the value of relationship is a good strategy.

Developing a positive relationship with yourself and others

will provide strength of mind and strength of character. When your centerbranch's relationship root runs deep, you'll find connection, comradery, and companionship—all valuable commodities when facing change. And if you approach every relationship you have with love, you'll find your greatest success with managing change.

CREATING CONNECTION

When I think back to the professional relationships I've had the privilege to develop over the years, some of my favorite memories go back to 2010 when I was working for Iron Mountain, which was a records management storage and shredding company. When I think about that team at Iron Mountain, I can't stop smiling—and it's one of those big stupid cheesy grin smiles, too. I can't help myself.

My Iron Mountain team was phenomenal. We had so much fun together. We still keep in touch, and as a matter of fact, I recently received a text message from one of my old team members. It was a group text that included nearly everyone on the team and had a picture of us nine years ago launching our very first project. The only person not included in the text was my boss at the time, who I forwarded the text to because we're still connected and doing side gigs together. We worked hard and we played hard, and those relationships will last the rest of our lives. That's the strength and connection that can come from nurturing relationships. They're valuable and irreplaceable.

Our team started with just two people. I was hired to create what was called Role Readiness Training. This solution was designed to successfully prepare hourly employees for their job in an appropriate and timely way. We started with our driver population because the company was turning over their drivers faster than they were hiring them.

The drivers had intense, high-pressure jobs. They drove to different companies to pick up boxes of highly sensitive documents and then transported them to a safe location. The chain of custody was critical to make sure we knew where those documents were at all times. While highly complex, in the simplest terms, if the customer needed the material stored in the boxes at a later date, the drivers would then have to deliver the appropriate boxes of material and return them to the company. Sounds easy enough, until you realize that a single warehouse can be over a million square feet with hundreds of thousands of boxes on shelves. And it was an employee's job to get the right box and deliver it to the right customer—all while maintaining the critical chain of custody.

Unfortunately, there were many instances where the chain of custody failed. The wrong material got delivered to the wrong company, and the drivers were overwhelmed with the process. None of them received proper training. Drivers would say things like, "Dude, you handed me a set of keys and told me to go pick up material, and that's all the training I ever got." It was a mess, to say the least.

My job was to put a team together to create Role Readiness Training for our drivers. At first, there were only two of us and the company told us, "We trust you, go and do."

We started the program with very little, but we eventually grew and built a training program, a peer mentor program, and a ten thousand square foot brick and mortar facility in Atlanta.

The building was our brainchild. We decided we would create a training center where people could learn to do their job in a safe environment. We had our own box truck and our own docks. When we implemented the program, not only was the company pleased, but the drivers felt more confident and capable of doing their job successfully. We changed the entire culture. We called it the Sentinel Program, and it's still in existence today. My team and I put in a lot of hard work and many long hours, in the end, it was a game-changer for everyone involved. The company saved tens of millions of dollars and we even won several awards. I attribute the success of the program to the fact that we bonded together as a team, and we created something amazing.

We valued our ability to connect with one another. We nurtured our relationship by having the hard conversations and challenging each other. We didn't always agree as we were building out the massive project, which was a multi-million-dollar investment for the courier program. Even with disagreement and challenges, everything was done with respect for each other. We had to get out of our own way to move the project forward. We were also passionate about what we were doing together and fully engaged in the work. It wasn't the same company with the addition of the Sentinel Program. And not only did it become a different company, we came out of that experience different people.

MAKING IT PERSONAL

A relationship is a partnership with shared values and complete respect for each other. This is what we strived for together at Iron Mountain. We worked incredibly hard and respected each other deeply. We all came to the team with different and diverse backgrounds and experiences. Rather than anyone thinking their experience or background was better than someone else's, we sought to really understand what every person could bring to the table. We each took our areas of expertise and drew the best from each other.

We made it a point as a team to encourage group thinking and made sure every single person's voice was heard. We also made sure to share in the effort. Because we were a small but mighty team, we all had different tasks to complete. If one person was done before someone else, we pitched in as a team, and all collectively crossed the finish line together. We always showed up as a team.

While I was the leader, we stood unified as a team—which you can only do when you have true relationships and deep respect for each other. And our relationship just grew from there. Those professional relationships became personal lifelines. We strengthened and supported one another both in and out of the office. We went to each other's family events and attended weddings together. They became some of my greatest friends.

We had the ability to thrive as a team because we made it personal. When one of us was having a bad day, we were there as a team with encouragement and support. This encouragement and support included three people volunteering to stay five hours late to help one person "dry run" their training session for the next day. It was one team member sending handwritten thank-you cards to every member of the team for remembering their birthday. It was my entire team rallying around me and picking up my slack and sending get-well cards when I was bedridden for eight weeks from an unexpected surgery. It was giving someone the extra time they needed off to grieve the loss of a loved one, and someone else not taking a vacation to cover that time. It was also celebrating the arrivals of new children and grandchildren. I could go on and on with the support that we gave each other.

When change happened to one of us, we strengthened and lifted that person through their difficult experience. I went through a divorce when I was working with this team, and it was incredibly difficult for me. I was not just grieving the loss of a marriage, but also coming to terms with the fact that I could not have children. During that time, one of my peers came to my house that I was renovating (after my divorce) and helped me paint. She offered to just come, help, and drink wine with me. It was a silent gesture of support that nourished my root of relationship because I had been withdrawing and slowing disengaging. By her showing up for me, it reminded me that relationship is the best way to get through anything. And while we were work colleagues, not friends, it made it even more impactful.

That kind of personal relationship allowed us to work better together as a team, and the outcome was a program that exceeded everyone's expectations. We moved through the major shift in the company and helped our couriers move through that change with greater ease and less conflict because of the value we placed on relationships.

We've all heard the phrase, "It's not personal, it's business," or at least some form of it. In my opinion, this is so far from the truth. If we take ourselves, our personal connection, and our relationships out of business, that business will crumble when major changes happen. Think of the many businesses that were able to stay afloat during the COVID-19 pandemic. Many of them were lifted up and carried on the backs of their loyal customers and employees. Everything from rallying people for support, to customers buying from them online, to creating GoFundMe pages, to employees willing to take less pay so everyone could stay on the payroll.

Many businesses are still around today because they made their business personal. I think of my current company—Collins Aerospace—who stopped manufacturing some of our aerospace products to start manufacturing face shields to fight the pandemic. We put our 3D printers to work making an overwhelming amount of supplies to be shipped to healthcare workers all over the world. One segment of our business even stopped making the fabric plane seats, and used the fabric to make masks and uniforms for essential workers, instead. This reengaged an entire population of people.

This is the perfect example of developing lasting relationships that keep people connected and caring for one another.

Another example of a company valuing relationship is a commercial automotive company in Chicago that has been kept afloat during a really trying financial time due to the care and compassion of the organization's leadership team. The CEO forwent his salary for nearly a year to make sure the company had enough funds to pay the rest of the staff. While the company isn't out of the financial dark woods yet, they are well on their way. And the team is hard at work caring for each other as they follow the example given to them by their leadership team. Their centerbranch was rooted in relationship, and that made a huge difference to their survival.

Never underestimate the people part of your business. Those relationships will strengthen you and help you to continue to grow, even when major shifts change the layout of your organization.

WE ARE NOT ALONE IN THE WORLD

Whether you're reading this book for personal or professional reasons, the relationship root of your centerbranch will be a huge benefit to your overall growth. The need for connection is a natural human tendency. We need it like we need air, food, and water. We need it to combat loneliness, to give us a sense of community, and to meet people who can challenge us to be better than we are. Relationships help us to grow, especially when we're faced with change.

Connecting with others gives us a different set of eyes to see things we may have never seen before. That new perspective can serve as a launching point for us to see the positive possibilities that can come from change, rather than focusing solely on the hardships brought on by it. Connecting with others can also help us recognize just how much we can rely on each other to get through difficult things. When the world starts spinning and chaos seeks to consume us, it's the people around us who will help lift us through the change.

I will never forget the people who stood on their balconies in solidarity during the quarantines of COVID-19 and sang together. For that single moment in time, they connected to each other and they lifted one another in their hardship. They stood alone, yet they sang together. They were many blended voices, yet they sang one song. We may all be different, but through valuing relationships, we can recognize how we're all very much the same.

Now, especially more than ever, there's so much loneliness in the world. I've been that person, sitting at home on a Saturday night, scrolling through social media all by myself. Sometimes we choose that, but it shouldn't be our norm. If we move back to people-centric and value relationships, we'll have a greater ability to stop the loneliness from spreading and maybe even come to the rescue of someone else. Loneliness should never be a thing. There are billions of people in the world. All it takes is strengthening your relationship with just one person to deepen your roots and help keep you standing in a storm.

OUR TAPESTRY OF LIFE

Every relationship you strengthen, you add another colorful thread to your personal tapestry of life. Too many times, we go through life with our heads down, our eyes shut, and our ears closed to the people around us. When we stop engaging with the people around us, we inadvertently stop creating the picture of our tapestry.

Every tapestry is uniquely different and beautiful, and it's our experiences with others that make up that tapestry. Tapestries are interesting in the fact that the beautiful picture can only be seen from the front. If you were to look at the tapestry from behind, it looks like a major disaster. It's messy and seemingly unorganized. There are strings and knots everywhere that are haphazardly tied together—like a cat got into the string and made a complete and utter mess with it. But turn it over, and you see how the haphazard connections on the back create a big picture that is stunning to behold.

I think our relationships are a lot like a tapestry. Sometimes they're messy. Sometimes things are knotted up and you have to work through and follow the thread to come together. And sometimes you need a new color to complete the picture you're creating. When you're engaged in helping one another and strengthening one another, no one comes out better than the other. Everyone has an important part in the tapestry. Together, everyone's colorful personality creates a breathtakingly beautiful picture on the other side.

That's the beauty of relationships. We can choose to look at the messiness of it all, or we can choose to focus on the beautiful picture on the other side. It takes a lot to see, and you may not see it right away. If you make it a point to recognize how each relationship adds to your tapestry, you'll start to see the world differently. You'll come to recognize that every single person you meet plays an important part in your personal tapestry and you play an important part in theirs. And together, you can create an impressive tapestry of your own.

When I think about what we created at Iron Mountain, this is exactly how it worked for us. Sometimes it was messy and sometimes it was confusing. But because we had our eyes on the bigger picture, never once did our threads unravel. Instead, we created something really special—both for the company we worked for and for our personal lives.

We began our tapestry ten years ago, and we're still working on it. Oftentimes, a tapestry will depict an image that will change and expand over time. Ten years later, I've formed some of the best relationships I've ever had because of the work we did together. Those tapestry threads represent all of the incredible moments we've had together. Like when one of the members of the team invited a group of us to his daughter's wedding in Boston. We all had to travel to go to the wedding—and it wasn't even a consideration. While we didn't know Bob's daughter, we knew and loved Bob, and we wanted to show our love and support for him. There were several couples who made the trip and we bonded as a team and as people. It was a wonderful experience and one that I would do ten times over again.

Those tapestry threads also include moments with my team that came far after I moved to a different company. When I was disillusioned because of the difficulties I faced in my new environment, four of my former colleagues from Iron Mountain met me at an industry conference. They took me for drinks and stood by my side—listening, reminding me of my past successes, and filling me up again.

These incredible people have been with me through many difficult changes in my life. And many times, they've been lifelines to help me see things from a different perspective. They challenge me and strengthen me to stand tall in the time of a storm. These are the beautiful people who have brought depth and color to the tapestry of my experience.

When we make the choice to engage and create relationships, we may be surprised and even delighted to see where they lead.

BATTLING DISENGAGEMENT

When I first stepped onto the corporate scene, before my Iron Mountain experience, I entered young and disengaged. What I mean by disengaged is that I didn't know how to engage appropriately in a professional environment. I thought having a job meant going to work, coming home, and going back to work again. And while there's nothing wrong with this approach to work, I didn't realize that there was so much more to experience if I engaged in actual relationships.

I watched my parents go to work and come home and they didn't seem to ever talk about anyone at work (at least in a positive sense), nor did they really "hang out" with anyone from work. I thought this was the only acceptable way to relate to work experience. It made me uncomfortable to go to happy hours, I hated "small talk" (actually, I still do), and I didn't know what to talk to people about—so I disengaged.

Additionally, I was also disengaged with feelings. Because I had only mastered one emotion, anger—and I knew enough to know that was not appropriate for a work environment—I didn't show any real emotion when I entered the workforce. Coming from a very poor blue-collar family, I didn't even know what "corporate" meant. Overall, I was disengaged as a child and adolescent, given my difficult upbringing, and I took that into my corporate life.

Disengagement may look different for everyone. Essentially, when someone is disengaged, they aren't giving their hundred percent effort. This was certainly the case for me. My heart just wasn't in it. I did my work and that's where it ended.

Because I came into the corporate world disengaged, I took the same approach with my bosses and coworkers. I engaged in the work, but I was disengaged with everything and everyone else. It was as if I had built this invisible wall around me, and if people got too close, I would immediately disengage. If I were a kingdom, it's the equivalent to lifting the drawbridge and putting fire in the mote so no one could ever reach me.

I have, to this day, only accepted one or two Facebook requests from coworkers. That is a fundamental rule that I follow. Others will likely disagree. That said, when people would get too close—i.e., want to hang out outside of work or invite me to things—I would politely decline (over and over again) until they eventually stopped asking me to go. Ironically, then I would complain that no one liked me, or I was excluded from the group. If someone got too friendly, I would become cold and distant with people in an effort to keep them afar. I know, now, this was driven from a fear of losing people or a fear that people wouldn't like the person they got to know, so I avoided it at all costs. It's all childhood wounds that I have worked, actively, to overcome. Yet, in my early career years, I didn't know what I didn't know.

I got a lot of tough feedback from people because of my disengagement. To be honest, the feedback hurt. I was told I was buttoned-up, unapproachable, and stoic. I didn't want this to be the image people had of me, but I didn't know how to change that image, either. I felt stuck and completely out of my element. And because I had no one to walk me through it, I fumbled and failed more times than I'd like to admit.

I didn't know how to act appropriately in meetings or other corporate settings. Rather than engage, I would retreat, and I would become much more reserved. I could only go off of what was familiar to me. And because I never shared personal experiences with my family, why in the world would I want to share them at work.

I was also told that I was reserved and hard to connect with and that I needed to start sharing and be more open with people. Because I wanted to reverse the image people had of me, I began sharing everything, which just made the problem worse. I had to learn the balance between sharing and over-sharing in order to manage the change I was constantly faced with. It wasn't easy, and I never felt that I could fully engage in that company.

It wasn't until Iron Mountain that those walls really came down. To be fair, I'm pretty sure that in the beginning when my Iron Mountain team started working together, I was still all of those things I had been accused of. Once I realized we were all a like-minded group of people, and that the group was filled with really good and genuine people, I changed my approach, which changed our work. I chose to love and to trust and to nurture my relationship root. I did this by deciding to engage, not just in the work, but in the people I worked with. This made all the difference then, and continues to make all the difference now.

So, how do we engage in relationships? How do we get our employees to engage in relationships? My answer to you comes in the form of another story about a tree.

THE ASPEN TREE

The Aspen tree is a unique kind of tree. When you look at a grove of Aspen trees, it looks as if there are thousands of individual trees that are growing side by side in a ginormous grove. But if you were to look at the roots, you'd realize that it's actually just one tree sharing a single root system. And what's even more amazing is that when any part of the Aspen tree needs help and nourishment, the other parts of the tree come to its rescue.

The largest living organism on earth is a grove of Aspen trees called Pando. The tree covers one hundred acres in Utah and is considered to be forty times heavier than a blue whale. It's also the oldest living organism, believed to be over 80,000 years old.

There's so much we can learn from this incredible tree that has outgrown and outlived every other organism on earth—and the lesson comes from its roots. Every tree in the hundred-acre woods are interconnected with one another because of what they're rooted in. And because they share the same roots, they are able to come to the rescue of each other.

In order to nurture relationships, it's important that we find commonality in our root system. Now this doesn't mean that if we're rooted in different things, we won't be compatible. But it does mean that the more we're rooted in the same values, especially in values-driven leadership, the more likely we'll be able to grow ourselves and our company through change. It also means that although our branches may go in different directions, our roots stay the same.

When we surround ourselves with people who have a similar values system, we can become a support to one another. And when our centerbranch is rooted in relationship, we're able to come to the rescue when someone is in trouble because we understand who they are, and we know where they're coming from.

Imagine, for a moment, this hypothetical example: perhaps you co-own a company and you are trying to grow your business. Let's say you have been successful to date; however, the next phase is to expand services and grow sales. If one partner is rooted in relationship, they may choose to empower their employees and give them incentive to make more sales or develop new services. If the other partner is rooted in financial gain, rather than relationship, they may be more demanding and drive the employees to harder targets without taking into consideration how to engage them in the process. If there is a disconnect on how to manage the team, and/or what direction to go in, the team will feel it as much as the partners feel it.

Ultimately, it becomes difficult to move the company forward because the energy is spent on the differences in how to manage. When the energy is spent there, disengagement will brew, and the original goal of new services and sales is unconsciously put on the back burner. Another downfall of this challenge is that the partners potentially risk disengagement from each other and the company may ultimately be at risk when this happens. Real growth can only happen when everyone is working together for the betterment of the company.

Pando is the oldest and largest organism because every individual Aspen tree is a part of the whole. They share the same roots and a common goal—to strengthen and support each other. Because of this, each Aspen thrives as they multiply and grow together.

If we want to strengthen the value of relationship personally, or professionally, the best way to accomplish that is to build on common ground. Find what connects you and hold onto that. This can be as simple as engaging in nonwork-related conversations to determine common interests and shared values. The same thing is true of a work project. Talk to your team members and agree on a charter or set of collective goals. Make sure everyone has a say in the outcome and revisit it often. In both scenarios, this sets a foundation for people to come back to when things get tough. It's kind of like home base when you are playing tag as a kid. Home base is always safe, and everyone can come back when they need to.

Work together to define a new goal that everyone can agree on. When goals are defined together, there's accountability there. Sit down and decide together what you want to accomplish, and then figure out how to hold each other accountable. Lift each other up to collectively meet the new goal. Learn from one another, and make it a point that when you see someone in trouble, you always come to their rescue.

Pando is the story of all of us. We were never meant to be isolated beings. We're all connected to one another. We're all interdependent and a part of the greater whole. We need each other. And when we finally come to that understanding, we'll all grow together.

Once we understand the power of connection, and we see through the eyes of love, relationships come naturally. We'll naturally seek to know and understand the people around us. And the more we come to know them by nurturing our relationship root, the more natural it will be to love and trust them. It's a natural cycle that keeps on growing and increasing the good you can experience through the commodity of true human connection.

PUTTING IT INTO PRACTICE

1. Make it a point to genuinely ask a coworker or loved one, "How are you?" You may think that this is quite basic. However, when we usually ask this question, we don't take the time to listen or allow others the space to *tell us how they are really doing.* I found this to be true multiple times in the face of COVID-19. Ask the question, and mean it.

2. Practice curiosity with people. Whether you've known someone for years or you're just meeting a new person, ask them three open-ended questions from a place of curiosity to build a relationship. This will help people to feel much more engaged.

3. Vulnerability isn't a swear word. It's one of the best leadership traits you can have. Allow yourself to be vulnerable with someone this week.

4. If you're in a virtual meeting, use your camera and meet face to face. It discourages multitasking and encourages connection and helps to build relationships.

5. When you're in a meeting or communicating face to face, be present and engaged in the moment.

6. Invite somebody to lunch. You don't have to buy it for them, just spend time with them and get to know them better.

7. Implement a policy in your personal life where you put your phone away for ninety minutes and connect with another human being without technology.

8. When you're walking by people, look up and make eye contact. Smile for goodness sake. Practice doing this for one week. Then practice for another week, and then another, until you make this a habit. It will change how you relate to people and how they relate to you.

9. Any time you feel disengaged during the day, track when it is and what's happening at that time. Find the trends that are leading to your disengagement. Once you've discovered the cause, make adjustments.

10. Have a virtual wine or coffee date. Create connections that have nothing to do with work. You could even join a life group. This will give you a lifeline of people you can lean on when loneliness and isolation set in.

CHAPTER 5

TRUST VS. CONTROL

"The best way to find out if you can trust somebody is to trust them."

—ERNEST HEMINGWAY

No one can deny that our world is changing. Living through things like terror attacks, natural disasters, economy crashes, and worldwide pandemics, it's easy to see that there will be times in our lives where we have very little control of the circumstances around us. Let's take COVID-19 as an example. In a matter of days, everything we had been accustomed to was taken from us. There was no visiting family and friends, no eating at restaurants, no attending sporting events, concerts, operas, plays, or even the movie theater. No extracurricular activities, no walking along the beach, no traveling or exploring, and absolutely no shaking hands with anyone. There was no going to school, no going to work, no going to church, and no going shopping for anything other than groceries. It was like an apocalyptic movie that was being acted out right before our eyes. Life as we knew it changed—and we had no control over it, or the consequences that would come because of it.

Any change is extremely difficult to begin with. It doesn't come naturally for most of us. When the changes come one after another, like a mighty hailstorm, it gets hard for us to wrap our brain around it. In order to hold on to some semblance of normalcy, our immediate response is to control the situation. And because there is little we can do, our need to control leads to a whole lot of worry.

In instances like these, it's impossible to control the outcome. There are just too many variables. We have to learn to let go and trust the process. Even if the variables are relatively few, rooting our centerbranch in trust will change the energy of our life from a state of perpetual fear to a state of quiet peace.

THE DANGERS OF A MICROMANAGING CONTROL FREAK

Because of the way I grew up, I didn't have a good understanding of what trust was, or why it was even important. I didn't trust people, in general, and I took that perspective into my career. I especially didn't trust what people could do; I experienced a lot of grief because of it, and so did the teams I managed. Because I was rooted in control, rather than trust, I believed that no one could do the work like I could. I would swoop in, take all the work for myself, do all the work by myself (working up to a hundred hours a week), and then pat myself on the back. I thought this was the best way I could control the work that was coming from my team. In reality, I was diminishing everyone else around me and overworking myself. The need to have control was derailing my relationships and ultimately controlling my life.

My work relationships especially suffered because of this. No one wants to be a part of a team where their contribution isn't valued or even accepted. I didn't realize what I was doing. No one told me to my face what they thought of me, but I heard the rumors. Word spread that I was a micromanaging control freak who didn't trust anyone.

I didn't believe the rumors, at first. I said to myself, *"No, this can't be. There's no way people are thinking this about me."* After all, my contributions were what made our team an asset to the company. But after I reflected on myself and my actions, I almost fell off my chair. They were right. Memory after memory flooded my mind. It was all there—in black and white. I *was* a micromanaging control freak. The rumors weren't rumors. They were the ultimate truth bomb that rattled my foundation.

The mirror was put in front of my face, and I saw the reflection of who I had become. With an undeniable realization, I started questioning how I got there. Because I couldn't control the big things as a child, I was determined that as an adult, I would always have the last say. Rooting myself in control had given me a false sense of security. I mistakenly believed that if I had control of everything, change wouldn't affect me. In the end, all control did was exhaust me and keep me isolated.

CONTROL BREEDS A CYCLE OF MISTRUST

This experience brought so many revelations I never recognized before. A lack of trust leads to our need for control. And one way it often shows up in our lives as micromanaging. The more we try to control the world around us, the more we believe that it's up to us. We start to think that we have the power to control the outcome of every choice or decision we make. And the more control we seek, the less we're able to relinquish control and trust others to make decisions on their own. We mistakenly believe that we're the only person we can trust.

Not only is this a damaging way to think for our own sanity, but it just breeds a cycle of mistrust. Through our own actions, we're telling people that we don't trust them. And while we may not come out and verbally tell someone that they can't be trusted—actions speak louder than words. People are going to know you don't trust them, and once they catch on, you've lost all credibility with them and they'll stop trusting you.

Why? Because people want to feel trusted, and they want to know that they can trust you. On the flip side of that statement, no one wants to feel controlled—no one.

Whether you're in a personal or professional setting, if you choose control over trust, people will slowly pull away from you. From a professional standpoint, employees will either quit or stop trying hard—they'll stop giving it their all. From a personal standpoint, people will either disconnect or leave the situation altogether.

If people pull away from you on a regular basis, consider your actions. Ask yourself the hard question. Are you addicted to control? Having completed this activity myself, it's both surprising and enlightening what you can learn from it.

CONTROL IS NOT A SUPERPOWER

Did you know that a person can get addicted to control?

I've seen my own addiction to control rear its ugly head multiple times throughout my life. As an adolescent and as an early adult, I didn't trust anyone. And because of this, control was my natural default. I'm not proud of this, and I cringe even thinking about it, but I used control as a sense of power.

In a personal setting with my family and friends, the more I could control, the more power I felt I had over the situation, or the outcome, or even the people around me. Ironically, the more I tried to control the situation, or the outcome, or the people, the more people would pull away from me. In the end, it was a losing battle. The only thing I gained was the knowledge that control is not power, and in fact, addiction to control is, in reality, a huge character weakness.

This character weakness can be severely damaging in an environment of change. In a work situation, controlling others, rather than trusting them to make their own decisions, creates an atmosphere of hostility. I've experienced leaders who try to control the outcomes and the decisions of people moving through the change, and it never ends well. I witnessed a leader once who couldn't stop himself from taking control of every aspect of the company. It started with a small group (my group) and then moved on to other aspects of the company.

In the beginning, he tried to control my actions, but couldn't, so he took control of my team and my function, instead. Rather than letting me run the training function, he went around me, worked with my team members, and directed them on what to do and what not to do. He even controlled how they would interact with me.

Once he had control of the training function, he turned to operations. He started showing up to operations meetings, uninvited, and would then take over the meeting. He barked out orders, and people were so dumbfounded that they just went along with it. When anyone would question his control or even why he was inserting himself—they were fired. Eventually, people just kept quiet and tried to keep their job.

He then moved on to the customer service group, and then the sales group. It actually became easier for him to control each group as he moved along, mostly because people were afraid. He viewed this as loyalty and that people trusted him, which was a far, far cry from the truth. As he took the work away from team members and gave it to people who he knew would do it the way he wanted it done, the work suffered because the wrong people were doing the work. Yet it became an addiction that he couldn't stop. And the more groups he would consume, the more power and control he felt he had. It was a vicious cycle that continued to spiral out of control.

The organization didn't perform well under those trying circumstances. The overall sales decreased, and there were multiple litigations that included a hostile working environment, age discrimination, and bullying. A lot of really good people left the organization, and those who stayed were hollow versions of themselves. There was crying in the stairwells more often than I'd like to admit. It was an awful experience. Change is hard enough without creating a toxic environment for your team members. This is why control must be weeded out of your root system.

If you're one of those people who is addicted to control—and you probably already have a good idea of who you are—it's time to let it go. I know you may think that being in control is your superpower, but it's not. And if you took the time to really search yourself, you would realize that control is wreaking havoc on your life and your relationships. Dig up the control roots that you've planted and replace them with trust instead.

Not only will relinquishing the need for control allow you to create a better environment in both your personal and professional space, but it will bring you greater peace in your life. You're probably thinking that I'm some sort of crazy telling you that if you give up control, you'll have peace, but I speak from experience and I know what I'm talking about. *Trust* me. There's that word again—*trust*. Learning to trust others will change your life.

DON'T LET CONTROL CONTROL YOUR LIFE

I used to think that peace came from my ability to control any situation. But the more I tried to control, the more my mind was swimming in all of the different scenarios and outcomes, working through mental contingency plans or what-if scenarios. I would spend hours and days and sleepless nights working through every possible outcome to make sure there was no scenario left unturned.

Every time I would try to relax, and especially at night as I was trying to go to sleep, my brain just wouldn't shut off. When I closed my eyes, it was as if an old-school filmstrip was playing in my head, forcing me to watch all the possibilities in which I could fail, driving me to come up with even greater plans to make sure I didn't. It was a vicious cycle and a damaging addiction.

I made it my mission in life to determine everything that could possibly happen and have a contingency plan for it. In my mind, peace of mind was the end result I was looking for. But there's no peace in that! It's exhausting, to say the least. And do you know the worst part about my madness? Ninety-nine percent of those scenarios NEVER happened. I wasted all my energy creating plans that were never used and never even necessary in the first place. Imagine what could have happened if I put that energy into something more positive. I could have built entire companies several times over with the energy I put into my imaginary contingency plans. What a waste of time and energy with nothing to show for it.

I know I'm not the only one who has struggled with this, but I'm here to tell you that you can overcome it. You don't have to let the need for control control you.

THE VALUE OF TRUST

Giving up control begins with our ability to root our center-branch in trust. For me, I planted my trust root when I found my faith and put things in the Lord's hands. While some people trust God, others trust the universe or any number of things that are greater than themselves. It can even be as simple as trusting your team members to make decisions on their own and giving them responsibility over extra work that would lighten your load.

However we choose to frame it, once we let go and give up control, we automatically reduce our mental and emotional stress. A natural consequence of reducing our stress is experiencing that incredible sense of peace that we all hope for. Our physical body will relax, and our load will feel lighter to carry. Instead of keeping our arms up, trying to balance all the balls in the air, we can actually physically rest—and it's glorious!

This is especially significant when we're moving through change. I've found that when I've relinquished control, and simply moved through change without forcing things into my own paradigm of what it should be, I've experienced the greatest growth and honest to goodness peace. In my work life, when I've trusted team members with greater responsibilities, they haven't let me down. More often than not, they've surprised me with their ability to meet and exceed my expectations—and we've both grown in the process. Trust breeds growth while control is a weed that chokes and stifles not only your own growth, but the growth of others.

TRUST BUILDS RELATIONSHIPS AND ENABLES GROWTH

When I was at Iron Mountain, working on the Sentinel Program, there was trust on every level. When my boss took a different role inside the company, I assumed her role. Because of the success of our program for training the drivers, the company came to me and asked if I would be willing to continue the work. They had actually lined up work for us that spanned the next four years that included creating training for the rest of their hourly population. This included training programs for our shred plants, for our document management professionals, and for our record center professionals.

They told me I would be reporting directly to the SVP of operations and then asked me if I would take the job. With this position came a new level of trust. It was an autonomous work situation where I would manage my own budget and supervise the progress on the project. I would travel when I needed to and give updates during our one-on-one. The SVP had so much trust in my team and me that one day he said, "All you need to do is let me know when you need me to remove a barrier or help you think through something if you're feeling stuck."

He trusted us, which gave us an incredible amount of freedom. This made us feel comfortable making tough decisions and even trying new ideas. We also felt capable. The company believed in our abilities to accomplish the work, so we more fully believed in our abilities too.

It was through that role that we were nationally recognized. Our work won award after award, year after year. Because of the trust we had with each other, we were nimble, and we were quick. We weren't bogged down with bureaucracy and we weren't waiting on approval from the top. It's uncommon for an organization to do what we did in such a short period of time, but we were able to do it because we collectively rooted ourselves in trust—from the SVP to the individuals on the team.

Because of that trust, we made an impact on the culture and the overall company. Together we reduced turnover and saved the company more than $16 million in safety accident and workman's compensation claims. It was unprecedented—all because of trust.

I never worked so hard and I never learned so much than I did in that role at Iron Mountain. I didn't know how to do the job, and I told them that when they hired me. But I figured it out along the way because I wasn't afraid to ask questions. I knew the company had my back and I had their trust. This made it a win-win for both of us. And together, we experienced growth.

When our centerbranch is rooted in trust, not only are we more capable of trusting others, but we're able to strengthen our relationships in every aspect of our life. And when we give trust to others, it's easier for others to trust us in return.

TRUST CAN BE LEARNED

Trust may not come easy to most of us. I'm not even sure if it comes naturally to any of us. We've all been hurt, betrayed, used, or abused. Believe me, it's not a value that I ever thought I could master. And there are times when I still have to remind myself to breathe deeply and just trust the process without driving the outcome. But the more we can intentionally choose to root our centerbranch in this value, the more successful we will be moving ourselves and those around us through change.

In my experience, trust has been one of the hardest roots to nurture because it goes against everything I grew up with. All I knew was control and relinquishing that control has been painful at times, and even scary. When I relinquish control, I have to trust in a process that may not yet be fully developed. I have to give up what I want something or someone to be, and simply let them be what and who they are.

Learning to trust is a line upon line endeavor. Start small and grow from there. Find small things that you're willing to let others take ownership of or make mistakes with. Find those safe bets that you can give someone to allow them to grow. It's important that when you give someone ownership of something, you allow them to do it their way, without reprimanding them for not doing it the way you would have done it. Part of trusting is allowing people to be who they are and use their own intellect, talent, and effort to complete the project. You may even be pleasantly surprised at the results.

Learning to trust is a daily endeavor. It requires you to constantly remind yourself not to look over someone's shoulder and micromanage their every move. It's a choice that you're going to have to make every day, maybe even several times a day. But when you make an honest and consistent effort, it will eventually become a habit. It will also be one of the greatest things you can do for yourself and the other people in your life. Remember, we all want to be trusted, and we all want someone we can trust in return. Be that someone by rooting yourself in the value of trust.

We have to stop trying to control people and circumstances, especially when change is at our doorstep. When facing change, trust is an essential root; we all have to move through that change together. Learn to trust others, and assume trust as well. I promise it will make all the difference.

PUTTING IT INTO PRACTICE

1. Name three things that you are currently/actively trying to control. For each of those things, create two columns and answer these questions: Why are you trying to control them? What happens if you trust someone to help/do them/etc.?

2. Answer this question honestly: Are you addicted to control? If you answered yes—I applaud you for being honest. What is one small item that you can loosen your control on?

3. Think of a time when someone trusted you to do something that perhaps you were not equipped or ready to do. What impact did that have on you? How can you extend that same scenario to someone in your workgroup or life?

4. Ask your coworkers or direct reports (or loved ones) if they think you're a micromanager or have control tendencies. Note: If you don't want the answer, don't ask the question...and don't get mad at people for being honest. If the answer is yes, follow up with this question: What can I do to change this perspective? Action necessary—do what they say and check back in periodically.

5. Decide on four items that you are willing to give up control on to nurture your root of trust. Each week for one month, select ONE of those items and have a conversation with someone (team, coworker, friend, etc.) to share that you would like them to take more ownership, help, etc. with that one thing. Use the word TRUST in your conversation and then do not take control of whatever it is you have given up. Do this each week for a month. At the end of the month, jot down your trust wins.

6. Evaluate your "Say-Do" ratio. Meaning, are you DOING what you are SAYING and vice versa? One way to immediately nurture your trust root is to keep the Say-Do ratio at 50-50. If you say you're going to let someone else take ownership of a project or decision, then do that! Don't swoop in and take control. If you do, it swings the scale of your Say-Do ratio and weakens your trust root.

7. Identify a scenario where control gave you a false sense of security.

Looking back, how would you rewrite that scenario leading with trust instead?

8. If control is your default, think about the key people in your life and write down ten reasons why you should trust those people.

9. Who do you trust with your most sensitive information and why? If the answer is no one, why not?

10. Has there ever been a scenario where someone hasn't trusted you? How did that make you feel? Find one person that you don't fully trust and find ways you can extend that trust to them. Start small if you have to.

CHAPTER 6

INTEGRITY VS. DISHONESTY

"Everyone thinks of changing the world, but no one thinks of changing himself."

—LEO TOLSTOY

If I were to poll top businesspersons, I would bet that nearly everyone would say that they strive to be honest in both their personal and professional lives. Yet even though we strive to be honest in all that we do, there may be times where we believe that being less than forthcoming is better than the honest-to-goodness truth. Maybe we're afraid we'll hurt someone's feelings, or lose our job, or damage our rapport with people, or any number of reasons. Fear is a tricky thing. It can lead us to make all kinds of poor choices because we're afraid of the consequences of an honest answer.

I wholeheartedly agree that it's not always easy to be honest. But our dishonesty, even in the little things, shows a lack of integrity.

The value of integrity is more than just being honest. Integrity means doing the right thing every time, regardless of whether or not it benefits us. That's not an easy task, but it will strengthen our ability to endure difficult change. When our centerbranch is rooted in integrity, we know who we are, we know what we believe in, and we will not let circumstances bend or break us. We'll stand firmly rooted in the truth that we know.

We're all going to face opportunities where our integrity will come into question, especially during times of transition. During those times, we have to decide to live in integrity no matter what, so when those changes come, we've already made the decision of who we're going to be.

DECEPTION LEADS TO DECEPTION

For most of my career, I've worked with truly incredible companies, with leaders who have led with integrity. I've also witnessed leaders who chose dishonesty and deceit because being honest wasn't in their best interest. I've seen many good lives ruined over lack of company integrity.

For example, a colleague of mine was on a high potential track in one of the companies we worked for, which I'll forgo naming, for obvious reasons. Let's just call him Steve. Steve was very well regarded within the organization, and probably one of the smartest people I've ever met; he was also equally as difficult. He had control issues, and it was difficult for people to work with him.

Steve was heading up an assignment in our research center where our intellectual property was housed. We had high-end engineers engaged in coming up with ideas that would lead to all kinds of competitive advantages for the company. One of these engineers was a person we'll call Tom. During this same time, the company we worked for was considering purchasing another company. Everyone involved was required to sign a nondisclosure agreement because the new company was a publicly-traded company. However, the two companies were unable to come to terms on the agreement, so the deal never happened.

About a year later, Steve had been promoted to run one of the commercial business units for the corporation we worked for. During this time, Tom made an allegation against Steve, claiming that Steve encouraged Tom to buy and sell stock for the company we never purchased.

Tom made this claim because the Securities and Exchange Commission (SEC) had flagged him for purchasing stock for the company we were going to buy-out, and then selling that stock before the deal went south. Tom's wife was a stockbroker and he made a lot of money off that stock. In an attempt to take the searing spotlight off himself, Tom told the SEC that he had no idea what was happening, and that Steve was the one who told him to buy and sell the stock. Because of this, a whole investigation ensued.

Both the internal and external lawyers agreed that Steve did nothing wrong. He did not buy, did not sell, and did not breach his NDA. Tom was the one who **allegedly** committed the crime. It was rumored that because Tom held several patents, the company didn't want to let him go and take those patents to their competitor. The company needed a scapegoat. Steve was difficult to work with, so he was the perfect patsy.

The company CEO went to Steve's boss, who was an executive vice president and a lawyer himself, and told him that due to the results of the investigation, he needed to fire Steve for his involvement. Steve's boss refused on the grounds that Steve had done nothing wrong. He told the CEO of the company that he would have to fire Steve himself, because what they were doing was wrong. So that's exactly what happened. Steve was fired and Tom was promoted.

OUR NEED FOR INTEGRITY

Shortly thereafter, the company started investigating me. The investigation came on the grounds that I wasn't managing my team appropriately. Mind you, I had just received an "exceeds expectations" on my review and was given a promotion with a bigger paygrade. But they said they had some questions regarding my leadership and put me through several pain-staking months of investigation.

One day, I asked the HR Business partner, who was leading the investigation, why they were doing this to me, and his answer was infuriating, "We're hoping you just quit; most people would have by now."

Now, I'm not one to back down from a fight out of sheer determination and stubbornness. I stood my ground through it all. And at the end of the investigation, they told me that because of the results, I would not be getting my bonus. Of course, I promptly told them, in not so polite terms, that it was a bunch of baloney and that I would be getting a lawyer.

They backpedaled and gave me the bonus, but then their true intentions came out. They began to ask me about my interactions with Steve. They asked me if I knew anything about the investigation, if I knew why he was let go, and if I was still affiliated with him. At that time, I had no idea what was going on with Steve. He never said anything about what was happening to him. Still, they wanted to know what I knew and what I would tell others (outsiders) if ever pressed. It was implied very heavily, though never in writing, that I was to never speak of anything as it related to my investigation or the investigation with Steve. They essentially wanted me to lie if I was ever asked about the incident.

Because they are such a large conglomerate, this is how they did business, and they felt they were justified. There were many others who knew about the incident with Steve. However, it was believed by many that the company was able to either buy them off or coerce them into never speaking of the incident. I knew that if I didn't comply, in the end, I would either lose my job or be forced to deal with the constant watch of Big Brother just waiting in the wings to swoop in.

Dishonesty is never justified. It's important to remember that. Integrity means being true to yourself and staying that way no matter what circumstance you find yourself in. If you're not the same moral person at work that you are outside of work, you've compromised your integrity. And working for a company with no integrity will eat away at you if you continue to stay in that negative environment.

I had a decision to make. I had to decide if my integrity was more important than the security of my job. I also had to decide if I wanted to continue working for a company whose leaders were seriously lacking in integrity themselves.

I told them that I would not lie for them. Later that month, I left my job with no notice and a ten-page dissertation—I mean resignation letter on my desk. Afterward, there was some back and forth between the company employee relations lawyers who kept asking me how the company could make it right. They wanted to negotiate a severance that came with a non-disclosure agreement attached to it, banning me from ever talking about the incident again. I would have never been able to look at myself in the mirror again if I had signed it, so I refused. I walked away from everything—but I still had my integrity.

When it comes to integrity, my greatest advice is this: Never be willing to sell your soul to the devil for better pay and a corner office. Your soul is worth much more than that.

CHOOSING OUR MORAL COMPASS

It's hard to choose integrity when you see dishonesty happen, especially in a large corporation. It's easier to look the other way out of fear. But when we choose to look away rather than speak up, we're ultimately condoning it, even if we didn't participate in the dishonest act ourselves.

We can choose to look past things we know aren't right—the things that eat us up inside—or we can do what we know is right and live our lives with integrity. When the integrity root of our centerbranch runs deep, our values become an intrinsic and defining part of our life.

Part of living a values-driven life is being willing to stand up for what we believe in regardless of the consequences that might come. It's our values that keep us centered, root us deeply, and drive our growth. If we fail to root ourselves in integrity, when life's storms come, we'll be tossed about like an unanchored ship on troubled water. And no one will be there to come to our rescue.

If we're not living with integrity, we're not being true to who we really are, or the person we could be. Unless, of course, we're a corrupt and dishonest person. If that's what we choose to root ourselves in, then we're being true to who we are, yet very few people will like us. I can tell you right now that if this is how we choose to show up in the world, the people who are drawn to us will be corrupt and dishonest too. Sadly, we'll never be able to trust anyone, and we'll always be looking over our shoulder for that person who's coming to stab us in the back. Because you and I both know that they're going to be coming.

Those who choose to root their centerbranch in dishonesty rather than integrity come across as a sleazy car salesman. We all know the type. They're shady and have a fraudulent air about them. This is because they can't hide what they're rooted in. And at the end of the day, those things will come to light and no one will want to work with them or be associated with them. If this is you, stop what you're doing and choose to be honest with yourself and others. Do it because it's the right thing to do. There's a reason why lying under oath leads to a prison sentence. It's wrong. Rather than weaving that tapestry I talked about in the previous chapter, you'll end up with a web of lies and deceit that will completely unravel when change happens.

We can't have integrity and be dishonest at the same time without ultimately losing in the end.

DRAWING YOUR LINE IN THE SAND

I'm a very visual person, so when I think of the proverbial line between dishonesty and integrity, I conjure up the image of someone actually drawing a line in the sand. I can see the waves coming in and erasing that line, and then the person drawing the line again. But each time the waves wash up and erase the line, the line is never redrawn in the exact same spot.

This is how I imagine it is for us in our day to day lives. We don't wake up one day and completely change our belief system regarding integrity. A change from integrity to dishonesty is a gradual one. We all have our values. But when those values are challenged, we may choose to draw our line differently to accommodate someone else, or sometimes even ourselves, depending on the situation. We'll tell ourselves, "This is my line. This is my go, no-go zone—my do, or do not." Then, when this line is challenged or someone crosses it, we redraw the boundaries.

When my ex-husband and I were married, he was a terrible husband and I was a terrible wife. I would tell myself, *"If he speaks to me inappropriately or emotionally abuses me one more time, I'm going to leave."* Then he would emotionally abuse me by telling me I was lucky that he married me since I had such a giant nose and ears. Or he would tell me that my butt was so big he wondered how I got up the stairs. At first, I would take it without even challenging him.

After a while, I started to fight back and for every emotional jab he threw my way, I slung one right back even harder. It was tumultuous, sad, and rooted in emotional trauma; yet I never left, which was my line in the sand. It's like the wave would wash up and move that line and I'd redraw another one because I couldn't do it. I didn't change my behavior, so he was never held responsible to change his. I didn't hold him accountable in any way; I just resented him more and yelled back louder. My line just kept moving over time, until I realized I had to draw my line and intentionally protect it so that it never had to be redrawn again.

I'm certain that we've all found ourselves in similar circumstances, whether it's at work or at home. We'll draw our line and then continually move the boundaries because we're afraid to speak up and be honest with people.

Most people won't have a job where there's an alleged mass cover-up of insider trading, but there may be small things that don't align with your values and may cause you to question your own integrity. You may look past it because you don't want to cause waves and you just want to get the work done. You may look at it and think that voicing your opinion won't matter or look past it because it doesn't immediately affect you—but it does affect you, whether you realize it or not. The more you adjust your line, the more you're readjusting your moral compass. Eventually, your compass will point in a direction you don't want it to.

If you were to look at the line you've drawn in the sand, is the line still where it was when you drew it or has it moved to accommodate those things that come up in life? I challenge you to draw your line and fiercely protect it. Make the decision now to never compromise your integrity. Do the things you say you're going to do. This includes the promises you make to yourself. Too often, the person we're most dishonest with is ourselves. We don't follow through with our own values and those promises we make to ourselves intrinsically. Because of this, we're still compromising our integrity and moving our line in the sand.

A major part of living in integrity is simply being honest with ourselves and with others.

INTEGRITY REQUIRES TRANSPARENCY

Rooting your centerbranch in integrity is learning to live with the best of intentions. When you're experiencing change, especially in your company, it's important to be honest and transparent with everyone involved. I'm seeing the importance of this with Collins Aerospace as we recently announced a new company president, seemingly out of the blue. I should mention that the previous president was beloved, and this came as a shock to many in the organization. Oh, I should also mention that because of mergers and acquisitions, this was the third president in a three-year period. As I said before, we are in the midst of the greatest change we've ever known as a company, and transparency matters.

I've had long talks with our executives to help them recognize that when it comes to addressing the changes people are seeing and anticipating, they have two choices. They can say nothing and let people come to their own conclusions, or they can be honest with their employees and tell them what they know and what they don't know. In the first option, leaving people to come to their own conclusions generally leads to made-up stories and convoluted ideas that are often far worse than the truth. People will fill in the gaps with their own storyline. It reminds me of a "choose your own adventure" book. And in most of these scenarios, the company and its leaders will be made out as the villain. It will breed conflict and mistrust, and no one ever gets to wear the coveted superhero cape.

The second option is the much better one. The leaders of the company may opt to tell their employees that they don't have all the answers, and they are committed to transparency and keeping the lines of communication open as new information comes in. This shows an element of vulnerability and builds trust. There will be times, for a variety of reasons, when leaders cannot share all of the information. It's vital in these instances that you express this to your people.

It's often as simple as saying some version of, "That is information that we are not yet able to share, however when we can talk about it, we will absolutely let you know." Again, it is truthful and filled with integrity and transparency—all of which build trust. And just like that, without even knowing it, those leaders will be wearing the cape rather than the villain suit.

In the end, the second option is what my Collins executives decided on. The West Palm Beach office I sat in was unique in the sense that the former president sat there, along with our CFO, head of strategy, a small group of key finance folks, the strategic development group, and the lone HR gal—me.

This office was considered the "headquarters" and was a very small, very tight-knit, and very gossipy group of people. It was new, only a year old, and everyone who worked in that office was relocated there. It was also not going to be the headquarters moving forward, as the newly announced president was based in Charlotte—our *other* headquarters.

For a recap, Charlotte had been the official headquarters under a previous, previous president. Then the headquarters was in West Palm Beach under the new, previous president, and now it is back to Charlotte under the new new president. Phew—did you get all of that?

In a conversation with our CFO, I expressed to him the importance of getting the office team together and having a frank conversation with them about the fate of the West Palm Beach office. It was absolutely top of mind for everyone in the office, as almost everyone had been relocated there within the last fourteenish months.

The CFO had some pretty firm reservations since he didn't even have the information yet. This was all happening real-time, and the first inclination was to swiftly move into option one and say nothing. I coached him on choosing option two, to simply share what he did know and what that means for them as employees and for their families, what it means if they do or do not want to move again, and what he could and couldn't share.

The finance leaders brought everyone together in a large group meeting and addressed the proverbial elephant in the room, "Look, we don't know what's going to happen with this office in the long term, but here's what we do know...Here's what we don't know...And here's what we absolutely know for sure: On a case by case basis, we're going to work with you individually to make sure everyone is being supported." They had a lengthy discussion and the CFO transparently even shared his own concerns. At the end of the meeting, our CFO was wearing the superhero cape. I don't think he even knows that to this day.

This was an unprecedented approach, and certainly not the norm. Most companies don't say anything until they have a plan. But these people's lives were in limbo, and Collins made the decision to be completely transparent with them to help give them a sense of comfort and peace. I was amazed at the number of people who approached us after the meeting and said, "Thank you so much for that information. We realize you don't have all the answers, but it helped us figure out where we stand."

This kind of transparency is not only appreciated in the workplace, but every relationship can be strengthened through complete and honest transparency. I'm not saying you should tell your wife that she looks terrible in her red dress if she asks you *that* question. Transparency should strengthen marriages, not destroy them. I am saying that when you're struggling in a relationship, the greatest thing you can do is communicate with each other and be honest about where you stand. Relationships cannot grow without open and honest communication. And sometimes, like in the case of my own marriage, when you're honest with each other, you recognize that the best thing for both of you is to part ways and still remain as friends.

Whether it's personal or it's business, create an atmosphere where you can share ideas and learn to give and receive constructive criticism. This is how we foster and develop relationships. It leads to new ideas and new ways of doing things. It's how we learn and grow together. It's also how we develop, nurture, and strengthen our integrity.

LIVING IN INTEGRITY

Change is hard and change is messy, but when we're dishonest with one another, it becomes incredibly complicated, and conflict is sure to happen. We all value the integrity of others, and we need to nurture that same integrity within ourselves. When we live true to our values, we're living our lives with integrity.

Rooting our centerbranch in integrity keeps us grounded and gives us a clear vision of the direction we need to go. Whether we're the leader of an organization or the leader of our home, this is an important lesson to remember. With our moral compass intact, we will most certainly find our way through any storm that comes.

Integrity leads to trust, trust leads to better relationships, and better relationships lead to a greater capacity to love. Every root is connected, and each one strengthens the other.

PUTTING IT INTO PRACTICE

1. Answer this question honestly: Have you ever overlooked or ignored potential dishonesty with others in your life? If yes, how does that affect your own root of integrity?

2. Draw a straight line on a piece of paper and label it with something you feel a strong integrity about. This will represent your proverbial "line in the sand." For example, I may write down: *The values of the company I work for must match my personal values.* Now, redraw that line every time you've adjusted, reconsidered, renegotiated, changed, or ignored this statement, intentionally or unintentionally. Chances are you will have multiple lines. There's no judgment here. The takeaway is a question for you to ponder: *How many times will I move my own line and how can I strengthen my root of integrity?*

3. Answer this question: What kind of person are you when no one is looking? Is this person different than the person that shows up when other people are looking? Make a change that will bring the two into alignment.

4. Identify one action you can take this week to display an act of integrity.

5. Think about your current circumstances, personally or professionally. Is there a scenario or situation where someone you know is acting in dishonesty instead of integrity? What is one action you can take to address this situation?

6. What is the greatest sacrifice you are willing to make to ensure you are rooted in integrity? This is a tough question to answer and will take a tremendous amount of thought and consideration. Once you determine what the answer is, write it down on a piece of paper or make a note in your phone, tablet, etc. Revisit this monthly to reinforce your commitment to live with integrity. It's important to make this realistic. For example, I left a high-level job because the company didn't align with my integrity value. That might not be the right move for everyone. To make this actionable, it must be realistic to your situation.

7. Is there something in your life that you are currently being dishonest

about? How can you move into a place of integrity regarding that situation?

8. Some people live in dishonesty because of a fear of repercussions. If you are living in dishonesty, is it motivated by fear? If so, what resources do you have access to that can help you through that fear and into a place of integrity?

9. Write down a white lie, an average Joe lie, and a big bald-faced lie. Do you find yourself justifying the smaller lies? If you do, make a choice to recognize that they are all lies, and they weaken your root of integrity.

10. Write down your definition of what it means to be rooted in integrity. Share your definition with your team and loved ones and together make it happen.

CHAPTER 7

SERVICE VS. SELFISHNESS

"...when you choose the paradigm of service, looking at life through that paradigm, it turns everything you do from a job into a gift."

—OPRAH WINFREY

When I was young and still in college, I had several jobs at the same time to get me through financially. One job, in particular, stood out above the rest—a summer job that I held for two seasons. I hadn't yet joined the professional world, and my bosses up to that point had been grocery store managers. To be honest, I really had no idea of what a good or bad leader was. I didn't even really know what it meant to be a good employee.

The summer job was at a campground in Pennsylvania, working for eight dollars an hour as an office admin under the main office administrator. It was a large campground managed by a man named Joe Durso. Not only was Joe in charge of nearly sixty employees, but he also had responsibility of the governance and maintenance of all of the residents in the campground. It was a huge responsibility. I was obviously someone of little consequence, so I fully expected to walk in my first day and work with the main admin of the campground, Mary.

To my surprise on that very first day, I was welcomed by none other than Joe himself. "I'm happy to have you on board," he told me. He then sat down with me and explained the rules and regulations, outlined his expectations, and made sure that I was equipped with everything I needed to do my job well. I had never experienced that in a leader before, and even as a college student, it left an impression. I felt like a part of the team from the moment I walked through his door.

This was just part of Joe's M.O. He would always make it a point to check on people, not in a micromanaging sort of way, but to make sure we didn't need anything. He spent his days in the service of others. Whether it was facilitating a tough decision or working with residents, he was always looking for an opportunity to serve.

MY WISE SERVANT LEADER

A life-changing experience I had with Joe came the day before our biggest weekend of the year—Memorial Day weekend, which was the start of camping season. We were preparing to welcome more than a thousand people into our camp-ground, and they all had to have gate cards. The gate cards allowed campers to swipe their magnetic key card to bi-pass the security guard's booth and gain access in and out of the campground.

It was my job to manually punch the gate card codes into the gate card system so that the magnetic keys would be activated. It was no-brainer work. Although the work was easy, Joe told me how important my task was. He reminded me that if I didn't have them done by the following day, it would take residents longer to start enjoying their vacation. Even in this, his main focus was on the campers and their overall experience and ability to enjoy their vacation as soon as they reached the campground.

After Joe left me to the task at hand, I had only entered fifty codes before I decided to stop. It was terrible work, so I just stopped doing it. I didn't tell anyone I stopped, either. I had no desire to punch tiny little numbers into a key card machine all day long, so I spent my day doing other things instead.

When Joe came in at the end of the day, he asked me if I finished the gate cards.

"No," I said, "I stopped doing them."

"Why?" Joe asked. "Tomorrow is the busiest day of our year. We need to have those ready." I could sense that I did something wrong. Up until that point, I honestly didn't think I was wrong in not doing the gate cards. I was young and extremely naive.

"Can you help me understand why you stopped doing them?" he asked.

"Well," I said. "My eyes hurt."

Thinking back on this experience, I was probably hungover and didn't want to do something so monotonous. Now that I've managed my own teams for most of my career, if somebody would have said that to me, I would have reacted much differently than Joe. Joe was a pro. Not once did he yell or lash out at me—even though I probably deserved it.

"Well," he said, "I can understand that. But let me explain to you again how important it is that we get these codes finished. We want our campers to have the best experience possible while at our campground. If you were on the other side, wouldn't you want that as a camper?"

The words Joe said next shocked me, even as a lackadaisical college student.

"Let me help you get through this," he said.

A NEW PERSPECTIVE

Joe had an entire campground to get ready for Memorial Day weekend, and he stopped everything to help me. Even though I messed up, he didn't scold me. He didn't tell me to get my butt back in there until the job was done. After he finished his own responsibilities, he sat with me for four hours to finish the task before the influx of people arrived the next day.

As we sat there together, punching the tiny codes into the key card machine, Joe gave me advice that I will never forget.

"Someday," Joe said, "you're going to have a situation like this where somebody doesn't do what you need them to do. And how you respond and what you do because of that is going to make all the difference for them. What we have to do, ALWAYS, is serve people the best we can, but also hold them accountable. I'm disappointed that you didn't do what I asked you to do, but I also want to show you what teamwork really looks like."

Joe's perspective changed everything for me that day. His advice is the foundation for how I think about managing people. When I'm faced with a difficult situation, it's Joe's voice in my head reminding me that how I respond to those circumstances will make all the difference to the people in both my personal and professional life. I had no idea what a servant leader was; all I knew was that I wanted to be just like Joe.

Rooting your centerbranch in service will make you a kinder, more compassionate, well-rounded person. It will help you to see the needs of others when change comes and get your focus outside of yourself. When your focus is no longer on you, you will be amazed at all the good you can do and how easy it is to move from one change to the next. Service also allows you to move through change together. Moving through change as a team, with people who are rooting for you and your success, is much easier than trying to move through change alone.

When someone's facing change, the best thing you can do for them is to remember and repeat Joe's wise words: "Let me help you get through this."

When we choose to occupy our time and energy focusing on the betterment of those around us, the less selfish we become. That's the sign of a great leader.

YOU DON'T NEED A TITLE TO BE A LEADER

We can all be leaders. It's an intentional choice that we make.

People often misinterpret the word leader to mean they need someone to manage in order to carry that title. If you're one of those people, I want you to stop perpetuating that false definition. A leader is someone who has influence, regardless of whether or not you have people reporting to you. Most importantly, we should be a leader of self, first. That way, we can be a better leader for others later.

Being a leader isn't a title; it's a life fundamental. It's the way you approach your life and how you look at the world and the people around you. It's about how to give back and contribute to the greater good, whether that's through your company or in your home and community. Leadership isn't a job; it's the way you choose to live.

You can be a leader by helping someone solve a problem, or by sharing important information that could help someone else. You could foster a community of caring in your neighborhood or your workplace. You could make meals to feed the homeless, or teach a child to read, or visit the elderly, or write a hand-written note to a coworker, or any number of other things that make a difference in someone else's life.

Being a leader is greater than a job and independent of a title. It's a choice we make on how we choose to live. If we choose to root our centerbranch in service, not only will we be an effective leader, but we'll have the capacity to become a servant leader in whatever circumstance we find ourselves in.

TWO KINDS OF LEADERS

While it's true that a leader is one who influences, the way a leader influences can be either positive or negative. Every-one can be a leader, but not all leaders are considered good leaders. In my experience, there are two types of leaders: ME and WE.

ME leaders are the leaders who are constantly taking credit for everything, even if it's not their own idea. They're searching for every possible way to showcase their work or skills, and they don't care who they have to step on to do it. These leaders are ego-centric and self-serving. They lead with *I* in their sentences: "I did this," "I should get the promotion," or "I'm only going to highlight my portion." These people always have an agenda and the phrase, *What's in it for me?* is always at the center of it. They're difficult to collaborate with because they figuratively take up all the space in the room.

ME leaders also take all the glory for themselves. Often, they hoard all the work and undervalue their team. Because of this, ME leaders are often overworked because of the demands they put on themselves for accolades. Because they leave no work for others, their team struggles with shared opportunities to learn and grow. These ME leaders may be successful, but they're unlikeable because it's like working with sandpaper. Relationships and the environment that houses those relationships are incredibly rough and often hard to manage.

Sometimes ME leaders are disguised as WE leaders. They use the right words, have their team do all the work, but then take the credit or only showcase what they did when it really matters. I experienced a leader like this at Carrier. When she really needed something done, she would go to the team, explain the needs, give some general direction, and rush people along to do the work. Before scurrying them off though, she would masterfully complement them and build them up so they were excited to go and execute exactly what she needed. At face value, this seemed like fine leadership, except it was ME leadership covertly disguised as WE leadership. When the time came to showcase the work that other people did, and present it to anyone of importance, the words "we, team, and they" never were uttered. It was only "I..." followed by promotion after promotion. Eventually, people caught on, and most people left. Sadly, she was only serving herself.

WE leaders are the complete opposite of ME leaders. WE leaders choose service over selfishness. They are leaders who always share the credit, often giving the glory to their team. They share the work and equally share responsibility. When they share the load, everyone gets to pitch in, everyone is valued, and everyone gets to be heard.

These are the leaders who choose love over conflict, they put time and effort into their relationships, they lead with integrity, and they trust and are trusted in return. These are the leaders who move both people and companies.

An example of WE leadership is my current boss at Collins. She has been with the organization for twenty years and has a reputation of getting the most out of people, building amazing talent, and being a role model at providing opportunities of exposure for others. She, like the previous leader I mentioned, builds people up and gets them to do amazing work. The difference is that she doesn't do it with ulterior motive. She doesn't present the work as her own, she allows others on the team to have that opportunity to shine. When that is not possible and she has to be the face of a project, she makes every effort to let folks know that it was a team effort and her part in the success was simply to remove obstacles and provide support where needed. Everyone wants to work for this woman. I actually left Carrier to work for her. I try my best to always be a WE leader because she showed me the way by modeling it for me every single day.

When we root our centerbranch in service, this is the kind of leader we become—a servant leader.

THE BENEFITS OF SERVANT LEADERSHIP

Servant leadership is our ability to put everyone's needs at the forefront. This is a valuable key to our continued success. Putting ourselves in front of others, or even putting others above ourselves, will never create a win-win situation for anyone. But when we focus on the individual needs of everyone involved and support one another, we will have the ability to accomplish impossible things. Servant leaders recognize this. They also understand that a rising tide raises all ships equally.

Now I'm not saying that we shouldn't have our own goals. Goals are essential for growth. We should set goals and work toward them, but never at the cost of others. That's what makes us a good servant leader. We lead by example, and we never discount the people around us.

Because of their service approach, servant leaders increase engagement and are the drivers of change. They are deliberate and conscious in their actions. They ask for opinions, encourage new ideas, embrace feedback, and give encouragement. Their focus on others invites collaboration and participation. This drives creativity up and keeps people purpose-driven and mission-oriented. They inspire people to want to be a part of the change and help them see the bigger picture and how the change will benefit everyone involved.

Servant leaders increase engagement because they are engaged themselves. This was exactly how it was with Joe. He was engaged and there to serve me from the very first day I started working for him. I immediately felt like an important part of his team. It gave me excitement not only for the job, but for being his employee. He treated me with kindness and made me feel that I was a part of something great.

Because of Joe's service to others, he never had a lack of people who wanted to work for him. Joe had seasonal employees who came back year after year after year. They loved him and were loyal to him because he loved them first and cared about them, too. This is the kind of leader we should all aspire to be.

LIVING A LIFE OF SERVICE

For some, rooting your centerbranch in service will come naturally. For others, it will take time, serious effort, and intentional choices to move from a mindset of ME, to a mindset of WE. But the more you practice mindfulness of others, the greater your capacity will be to make it a habit in your life. Your ability to lead will increase because people will want to be around you and learn from your example. They will feel cared for, listened to, and important.

Joe's management style made me want to be a better person because he believed in me. I would have done anything for him because of that. No matter what changes we went through, he was there by our side, every step of the way. When we learn to lead like Joe, there is so much good we can do. Joe may not remember our conversation—he may not even remember me—but his example and the lessons I learned from him were so profound that twenty-five years later, I'm still talking about them. That's the impact of servant leadership. A seemingly insignificant event, punching numbers into a keycard machine with my boss, has led to a lifetime of choices.

When we're rooted in the value of service, our positive influence will be felt by all those we genuinely love and serve. This kind of leadership is vital during times of transition and change. When people are looking for answers and unsure of how to move forward, we'll be there to comfort them. In true

Joe style, we'll be able to confidently look others in the eye and say, "Let me help you get through this."

PUTTING IT INTO PRACTICE

1. Determine what kind of leader you are and what kind of leader you want to be. You may want to ask a few people this question as well; we often get this self-diagnostic wrong. As I mentioned before, don't ask if you don't want to know. It won't end well for anyone.

2. Ask at least one person a day for the next thirty days how you can be of service to them. Then follow through on that. Note: Don't do this if you cannot follow through. It will exacerbate your potential reputation of selfishness.

3. Identify one area of your life where you are selfish but shouldn't be; outline one action to reduce this. Note: It is completely fine to be selfish in some components of your life, like self-care and creating appropriate boundaries. These help you to be of service to others, too!

4. Think about the last time you had a big win, major success, or completed a heavy task. Ask yourself these questions: Were others involved/did others help? Did you acknowledge these people to others, noting their contributions? Did you take the glory or the win for the team because you are the leader? Did the team feel engaged and genuinely share in the success? Honest answers to these questions will help you to determine if you are leading for others or leading for yourself. If it is mostly about you, you may want to rethink your leadership style and nurture your root of service.

5. Instead of telling people your expectations of *them*, ask them what their expectations are of *you*.

6. In a team meeting or in a personal conversation, ask others to hold you accountable for being a service-oriented leader/person, and to call you out when you fall into selfish behaviors. You will get a theme here—don't do this if you really don't want to be held accountable. It will just irritate everyone.

7. Get a group of people together, either personally or professionally, and participate in a service project like Habitat for Humanity.

8. Make a concerted effort to treat everyone with respect in your sphere

of influence, regardless of their circumstances. This models servant leadership.

9. Create a situation where you can allow someone else to have the opportunity for leadership and exposure while you take the backseat. Let them showcase their talent and get the credit for it as well.

10. As a company, take a 360 Assessment to get unbiased feedback to help you identify what kind of a leader you are. Create an action plan from that data of how to be a better servant leader in your company. *A 360 Assessment, also called multirater feedback, is a process through which anonymous feedback from employees, subordinates, colleagues, and supervisor(s), as well as a self-evaluation, is gathered and presented back to the employee in a report format which outlines trends, gaps, and direct commentary.*

CHAPTER 8

JOY VS. COMPLACENCY

"We laugh to survive. Then, with joy we thrive."

—MARY ANNE RADMACHER

Nearly every dictionary defines joy as the emotion you feel when you have success or good fortune. This means that when you land that big client and go out with friends to celebrate, you're essentially experiencing joy. While I agree that these celebratory moments are joyful, success and fortune don't always bring joy, and certainly not the kind of joy that is lasting. Lasting joy is rarely about the best job, or the most money. The joy I'm talking about is so much more than that. I've had both success and fortune in my life, but still lacked joy.

Oftentimes, we're complacent and mistake it for joy. Complacency is self-satisfaction, which can be perceived as joy, but it's accompanied by an unawareness, or ignorance of our own deficiencies, and possible dangers. To be complacent is to become so pleased and comfortable with ourselves that we don't even put forth the effort anymore because we believe that we're just that good.

Complacency in the workplace can be equated to neglect and carelessness. A complacent person may neglect the detail, or put work forward that isn't accurate thinking, that it's fine. They're unaware of the realities that are around them. A complacent individual may become sarcastic or blaming, even confrontational or defensive when the rug is pulled out from under them.

Those who are complacent may feel momentary joy in their self-satisfaction, yet, over time, even they recognize that something is missing. They just aren't sure what *it* is. What they are missing is actual heartfelt joy. I know because that was me.

JOY ISN'T IN THINGS

When I started my corporate career, my first job gave me clout and prestige. I worked for a health and wellness company, LA Weight Loss Centers. And I didn't just work there, I was a client too. While working there, I successfully lost seventy-seven pounds—I was an overachiever on the Freshman Fifteen.

While at LAWL, I was on the cover of *Women's World* magazine,

I was featured in national commercials, and I was even a guest on *The View*. A normal person would have been elated to experience any one of these things. And while I was, in fact, elated, there was still a complete lack of joy. I often experienced a feeling of emptiness instead.

Now, don't get me wrong, I may not have had joy, but I certainly had a whole lot of other things—including plenty of ego. I was a fierce competitor, and it felt good to be a rising star. But those joyful moments were fleeting and only lasted as long as the moment itself. While I may have had success, a rapidly growing career, and more money than a twenty-something should have, there was no passion or purpose. I had everything I thought I wanted and should have experienced joy, but I just didn't. I mistakenly tried to use all that excess money to buy joy, but all I ended up with was stuff that I moved around for years to come, only to finally give it away in the end.

I was the textbook definition of complacency. I had self-satisfaction, especially from my weight loss, which made me arrogant, and essentially, an egomaniac. Neglect and carelessness led to me getting fired from that job and I didn't even know why. When they told me my role was being eliminated, I asked them why I wasn't being used to fill one of the other open positions. They just looked at me with a blank stare. I really didn't get it. I was unaware of the reality around me and never even sensed the danger of losing my job. I really saw myself as indispensable.

After I was fired, I wondered how I was going to pay for all the credit card debt that I had accumulated trying to fill that awful void that just wouldn't subside.

So, I moved on to another company that sold disaster recovery software. My job was in software solutions, which meant that I would demo the product for prospective clients, answer all of their questions, and pre-sell them. Then, once they were ready to buy, I would hand the client back over to the salesperson to sign on the dotted line.

I was a great pre-salesperson. I closed more business in six months than others had in three years. It's too bad that I made 1 percent commission and the sales folks made 10 percent. In that job, I met my ex-husband and some friends that I have kept in contact with for nearly fifteen years. It was a fun job that I was really good at, yet I had no joy.

I left that job when I was asked to help a former LAWL franchise owner start a new business. It sounded exciting and I managed to negotiate a great salary. Because I was making more money than I ever had before, I also had more expensive "things" than ever before. Sixteen joyless months later, the company went bunk when the '08-09 economic crisis hit. Same story…get a job…find success…buy things…experience a feeling of emptiness…rinse and repeat.

Eventually, I landed a wonderful job at Iron Mountain—which

I talked about before. While there, I had a great team and we received many awards for our work. I loved my team and valued our relationship, but I still couldn't find joy within myself. I was proud of the work we accomplished, yet I still had this emptiness inside. Thinking there had to be something more, I accepted a new job with Bridgestone Retail Operations in greater Chicagoland, who recruited me to fill their training need.

You know the story of this job. It was one of the most difficult challenges I have had to date, yet I was very successful in this job and accomplished the work better than anybody expected. I then transitioned to the Bridgestone America's headquarters in Nashville, where I had the privilege to run leadership and development for the company's 70,000 employees. While there, I worked internationally with our parent company in Japan to determine how to develop people globally. I was great at my job and found significant success. A very dear colleague and I even helped to build the country's very first bachelor's degree program in Applied Leadership in conjunction with the Military Academies and Middle Tennessee State University. We killed it with that program. It positively affected thousands of people's lives. Not many people can say they've built a bachelor's degree program. Still, there was not a whole lot of joy.

No matter what I did or which job I moved to, joy was a wily minx that was elusive and hard to find. I had plenty of self-satisfaction from my accomplishments, yet I wasn't aware of my own deficiencies. I ignored them, all the while choosing to focus on "things" to make me feel better.

LASTING JOY COMES FROM WITHIN

I knew joy was lacking in my life but couldn't figure out how or where to find it. One day, I decided to search myself and made an incredible discovery; Joy is not in things, joy is in us.

The kind of joy that goes beyond singular moments can't be found in big titles or shiny new toys. It's not sold in stores, nor is it on the cover of magazines. This kind of joy doesn't stem from things; it grows from deep within us. When we root our centerbranch in joy, it becomes a wellspring that runs deep and is ever-flowing.

Centering ourselves in joy isn't about gaining all the things we hope for. We can hope for things all day long, but circumstances and people change along the way. We may never get what we hope for, and if those things become the measuring stick of our joy, we may never find the joy that we seek.

Joy isn't found in some future event, or the consequence of attaining expensive things. Joy can be had right here, right now. And most often, we'll find it in the simple things that cost nothing at all.

As I continued my search for lasting joy, I pondered what it was that truly made me happy in life. I wanted more than joyful moments—I wanted a lifetime of joy. I wanted joy that would stay with me, even through the most difficult of circumstances. In my searching, I realized that serving others brings me the greatest joy. And that joy stayed with me long after those moments of service were over.

Since service was my avenue for lasting joy, I decided to start getting active in serving others and make it my life's mission. I asked myself the question: "How can I take the gifts that I've been given and the experiences that I've had and use them to impact other people?" This question led me to invest in my own business, known as Centerbranch.

Starting my own business was emotional and scary, yet it brings me joy at the same time. That's what makes joy so incredible—it can be intertwined with so many other emotions and isn't solely attached to happiness. With Centerbranch, the joy is coupled with a multitude of emotions, but joy is the greatest of them all.

I didn't understand what lasting joy was until I founded Centerbranch. I realized that every experience I've had and every job I've been recruited for was to help people and companies grow through change. Each experience has set me up to serve others as they face difficult experiences and tough transitions in their life. The goodness that came out of every challenging situation is that I was able to use that to coach or help another person who might also be struggling. The same thing is true of my successes—it is all in the spirit of serving others through my experiences.

When I'm coaching people and companies through change and speaking at corporate events, it's more work than I've ever done, but I'm actually less tired and more energized than I've ever been. The complacency is gone and for the first time in my life, I can honestly say that I experience a true sense of joy almost every day. I've found my passion and passion is the wellspring of joy. Sometimes it is overwhelming to experience, in the most beautiful way possible. I didn't find lasting joy until I started doing the work that mattered the most to me.

Rather than self-satisfaction, my satisfaction comes in helping others, and in knowing I'm making a difference. I put my heart and soul into my work, and the rewards that come from that is that I get to see other people make a difference in the world. My complacency for life has transformed into the deepest wellspring of joy, and there is no more void within me.

When we identify what we're passionate about and incorporate that into the work that we're already doing, it feels as if we're doing less work, and it becomes much more fulfilling. It may not be less hours, but we'll waste less energy, and it will feel easier because it's something we're passionate about. This is not a lightbulb moment, and it often develops over time when intention is adequately applied. That is how we root ourselves in joy.

Finding joy is a root we have to nurture—if it's not there to begin with, it won't grow on its own. We must find our passion and create an atmosphere of joy in our day to day life. In other words, if we find and do the things we love, we'll love the things we do. It's a mindset that will serve us well if we choose to employ it in our life.

THE JOY MINDSET

Having a joy mindset is more than just finding our passion; it's identifying our reason for doing the things we do. This mindset is essential when we're forced to move through change. When our centerbranch is rooted in joy, we stop looking for the problems in the situation and we start searching for the joy in it. We recognize that our joy is independent of any situation and is determined by our own choices and frame of mind.

Our joy doesn't come in things or circumstances—it comes in our own change of heart.

Let me give you a perfect example of what I'm talking about. I pay a woman, Adriana, to come in and clean my home once a week. Don't judge me in that. I'm a busy woman and paying Adriana to clean my house gives me more time to do the things I'm passionate about. And let's be honest, I've never been passionate about cleaning. Adriana is sincerely the most wonderful human being I know. She is also fiercely devoted to God. I love talking with her because I gain so much from seeing the world through her eyes. She has an incredible perspective on life. In one of our recent conversations, this is what she said:

"I clean houses because this is the job God gave me. One day I was feeling very frustrated because a client asked me to clean her toilet with my bare hands. She didn't want me to use gloves or to even use the toilet brush. She wanted me to get my head into the toilet and clean under the rim with my bare hands. I didn't want to do this, and I felt very unappreciated. I cried up to God and I felt Him speak to me. God told me that I needed to have joy even in cleaning a toilet. He said I had to repeat, "I am happy."

Even though I was NOT happy, I kept saying "I am happy." After a while of saying it, I actually was happy. God told me that no matter what I'm doing, when I do it with joy, I'm doing His work, and it will be good, and all will be well. This changed the way I look at my job, even when I'm cleaning a toilet. Now, I approach cleaning other's homes as a joyful act. Not only is it an act of service to the person whose house I'm cleaning, but I'm also in service to my God."

Now, regardless of whether or not you believe in God, the principle is absolute truth. This beautiful woman was passionate about her faith and the God that she serves. And because of this, she was able to find joy in cleaning other people's toilets. It's an incredible testament to what can happen when we find our passion and apply it to the work we're already doing.

Not only can this joy mindset change our lives, but it will change the energy with which we do everything else. Rather than becoming angry because we're put in a less-than-desirable circumstance, we can choose to find the joy in every situation. If this blessed woman can find joy in cleaning someone else's toilet with her bare hands, we can certainly find the joy in our own life's work.

"DO, GET, HAVE—HAVE, GET, DO"

I'm guessing that most people who are reading this book have experienced some kind of success in their lifetime. But here's an honest question for you that needs an honest answer: Are you happy? Are you experiencing joy in more than just the singular celebratory moments that come and go? If you're missing joy, I would suggest that it's because you're doing the wrong work, or you're seeking the wrong things in your life, or you've followed the wrong formula.

Most people in life use the formula: *Do, Get, Have.* In other words, we tell ourselves that if we *do* our job, we'll *get* X amount of dollars or X promotion, and we can *have* whatever we desire. We may even believe that once we *do* the job, *get* the money, and *have* the big house with the big boat and the fancy car that we'll be happy.

But ask any person who has ever won the lottery if that formula has worked for them. Having the money to buy whatever we want rarely leads to happiness. Once people have what they want, many still lack happiness and may even feel less fulfilled. Think of all the celebrities who have more money than they could ever spend, but still wind up unhappy. And nearly every time, their unhappiness leads to another round of *Do, Get, Have*.

It's a vicious cycle with very little success in finding the actual prize: joy. Additionally, we struggle to find peace in our lives because we put so much energy into *doing* and *getting* that it feels like the *having* never comes.

If you find yourself stuck in this vicious cycle, may I suggest a new formula? *Have, Get, Do*. Meaning, if we *have* joy, we'll *get* what we need to *do* what we love. It's really that simple.

Most people are approaching life backward by expecting that what we do, have, and get will bring us joy. When the answer to lasting happiness is to approach life with joy first, and everything else will follow. When we root ourselves in joy and determine what truly makes us happy, the rest will come much easier.

Joy is not something we achieve after we've exploited every opportunity. As I said before, joy is a mindset. It's determining what makes us happy and choosing to make that a part of our daily life. It's also finding joy in the work we've chosen to do, regardless of what that work is. It's looking at it, not as a means to an end, but as an opportunity for growth.

When we apply the formula of Have, Get, Do, we will have the ability to change the outcome of our own lives and positively influence the lives of those around us.

LIGHTING THE SPARK

As leaders, we need to be rooted in joy so that we can more effectively light the spark of others. It's our responsibility to make sure that the people within our organization are happy, engaged, and joyful. This doesn't mean that we need foosball tables, extensive time off, and free lunches for every employee. This isn't the kind of joy I'm talking about. Remember, joy isn't in things.

This is about talking with the people in our organization and making it a point to really get to know them and what makes them happy. This requires us to leave our office, walk around, and spark a conversation. Don't send an IM when face-to-face interaction is available. They won't care about the company unless they know they're cared for too. We'll do more for our company by understanding our people than anything else we can do.

We need to make an effort to know who our people are and what they're motivated by. What is their centerbranch, and what is it rooted in? By determining this for each individual in our organization, we can help each one find their passion.

Remember, a person's centerbranch is what you see, so start

looking. What do you see when you look at the people around you? What can you learn about their passions and beliefs? This can be discovered through regular performance and development discussions. But it can also be determined simply by having a genuine interest in our teammates, peers, and coworkers. It can be as simple as asking.

I recently had a conversation with a young finance professional who has spent a good portion of her career in complacency. She lacks any passion and really has no love for her job. When I sat down with her, I asked her the tough question.

"Why are you in finance?"

"Well," she said. "My dad told me it would be a great job."

"Do you even like finance?" I asked.

"Well, it's okay," she responded back. It was as if the only reason she was doing it was because her father told her she should, and she didn't want to disappoint him.

"What's your passion?" I asked. "What gets you the most excited every day?"

"Nutrition and health," she said. As she said it, her whole demeanor changed. She sat up straighter and smiled.

"Well," I said. "How can we incorporate nutrition and health into what you do in finance to help bring your passion into the workplace?"

We then sat together and discussed ways we could take what she was passionate about and apply it to the work she was already doing. Of course, it took some thinking outside of the box, but it lit a spark in her, and she started experiencing greater joy in the workplace.

Lighting that spark within her was as easy as asking a question and being willing to think outside of the box. The possibilities are really endless. And by asking questions, we may be pleasantly surprised at what we can learn.

DEVELOPING JOY

Helping someone find their passion and discover their joy is an interesting process. It's the most rewarding part of leadership, but also the most difficult and time-consuming. And because we live in a society where we have less resources, more demand, less time, and more distractions, there isn't a lot of time left over for developing people.

True leadership development happens in the trenches. It's hands-on, and it's personal. It's not a one size fits all approach. What brings out engagement and joy in one person might not be the same in another. It's like a jigsaw puzzle. We have to figure out what drives and motivates each employee separately.

We also have to learn to take our own biases out of the equation. What motivates us may not be motivating to someone else. For example, if a manager is highly motivated by money, that manager may want to give everyone a bonus. In doing this, the manager may believe that this action will spark happiness across the board. But if a person is motivated by recognition, or by quality time with family, the money isn't going to have the same effect on them. Sure, they'll be happy about the bonus in the moment, but the joy isn't going to be a lasting one.

Every person is different. And because it's highly individualized and takes serious time and effort, most leaders don't take the time to do it.

Even though it's time-consuming, we need to find the time to make it happen. Fostering joy is an essential element to keeping employees grounded through change. Without joy, the most you'll ever have is employees doing their job as a means to an end. And when change comes, they'll have nothing to hold onto.

If we intentionally pause to help others through development discussions, finding their passion, figuring out their center-branch and what they're rooted in, it's going to pay off in the long run. Those people are going to be more engaged. They're going to be more productive. And they're going to add positivity and joy to the work atmosphere, which is infectious and will spread to everyone else. They'll essentially pay their joy forward. Our efforts in joy development will require us to spend less and less time putting out fires, because there will be very few fires to put out.

When employees are happy with their work and find fulfillment in it, they are more likely to stay with the company and remain positive, even during transition periods. They will know what they're passionate about and understand where their joy comes from. They will recognize that joy is not about the circumstances they're in, but how they decide to face those circumstances with their own joy mindset.

ON A PERSONAL NOTE

Having said all that, there's nothing wrong with work being a means to an end. But with joy as a root, work and life can become so much more. When we see our circumstances with a joy mindset, joy will come back to us. That is how rooting our centerbranch in joy becomes a wellspring. Joy brings joy.

Without joy, life lacks meaning and it's a struggle to effectively move through life, let alone change. It's as if we're the walking dead, trudging through mud, ever searching but never finding what we're looking for. And in the end, the material things will never bring us the happiness we're looking for. All the money in the world isn't going to give us a hug at night.

When I was in my early years, I thought I had joy. But there was always a sense of being unfulfilled and I was always wanting more—more money, more prestige, more success, more accolades. No matter how or where I looked, I could never find my passion or experience the joy I was looking for. That is, until two things happened in my life: I leaned in and figured out what I was meant to do in life, and I found Jesus. That is where I found my greatest joy.

What brings you joy is most likely going to be different than what brings me joy. But the promise is the same—once you find your passion, it will change your life, and you'll never want to let it go.

Joy is possible for each of us if we do the necessary work to find it.

PUTTING IT INTO PRACTICE

1. Name at least three areas in your life where you are complacent. For each of those areas, make a list of ten reasons why you should move from complacently to joy and ten consequences if you don't.

2. When is the last time you belly-laughed at work or at home? How can you create more of this?

3. When you hear the word joy, what comes to mind? Make it a point to do more of that.

4. Think of one unexpected way you can bring joy or fun to your workplace this week, even if it's virtually. Now go do it.

5. Just before or after a potentially stressful meeting or tough conversation, take two to three minutes to recount a moment that has brought you joy or happiness in the last few months. Taking just a few minutes to reset your thought pattern and focus on joy is a great way to avoid potential negativity and complacency.

6. Ask three people this week what brings them joy and have a quick conversation on that topic with them. Choose one person and implement one thing you can do to help develop their joy.

7. Think about your daily routine. Is it the same or almost the same every day? If so, this tends to lead to complacency without even realizing it. What is something you can do this week to mix up your routine?

8. Numerous studies have shown that gratitude increases joy. Create a gratitude note on your phone or tablet or in a notebook by your bed. Before you begin each day, write down one thing you are grateful for. Do the same thing before you go to sleep. By the end of the year, you will have over 700 notes of gratitude. This doesn't have to be a brain-buster. This morning I wrote down that I was grateful for my memory foam pillow. That pillow is a literal game-changer for me.

9. Write down a list of the top ten things you're passionate about. Incorporate at least two of those things into your week. It really should be every day.

10. If you're in a place of complacency and you feel no joy, how did you get there? Unwind what brought you to the place you're now in and determine how you can find your joy again. Take steps to make it happen.

CHAPTER 9

SPIRITUALITY VS. NOTHINGNESS

"Change is painful, but nothing is as painful as staying stuck somewhere you don't belong."

—Mandy Hale

A mother who was dying of cancer asked her daughter to drive her to the ocean. As they sat on the beach together, the mother watched as the daughter looked out over the vast body of water. The mother softly leaned into her daughter and whispered these words.

"Do you see how impressive the ocean is? It extends as far as the eye can see with no end in sight. On the other side of that ocean, there is a whole other world to explore. And it's the invisible wind which powers the sails that will take you there. I brought you here to help you remember these three things:

The ocean reminds us that there's always something greater than ourselves. The other side reminds us that there's a reality beyond what we can actually see. And the wind reminds us that our faith in invisible things can take us places where we cannot reach on our own."

I love this story because it's a reminder of how seemingly insignificant we are, yet there's so much good we can do. Living with spirituality allows us to see the bigger picture and recognize our place in it. Not only is this important for individuals, but it's important for organizations as a whole.

Adopting spirituality in your life and your workplace will allow you to bring meaning, compassion, mental wellness, whole-self balance, and so much more to your organization. We each have different pieces of ourselves, our spiritual self, our private self, our sarcastic self, our business self, our relationship self, our church self, and so on. What if we showed up as our whole self? How much more impactful would that be? Allowing spirituality in the workplace will allow for whole-self integration. With it, everyone's life will be enriched by seeing the bigger picture and recognizing their place in it.

BE THE GOOD

We all need something greater than us to believe in. When difficult circumstances come, and our entire foundation crumbles, our belief in something greater will anchor us and give us the faith to endure the hardship.

Take the COVID-19 pandemic, for example. Many foundations crumbled when jobs were lost, toilet paper was scarce—which, by the way, I will NEVER fully understand, schools were canceled, and we were all confined to our homes. Near pandemonium broke out. Fear of the coronavirus was crushing people. We felt it in our corporations, in our personal lives, in the economy, and in the very core of our being. We watched the world change right before our eyes in real-time and across the entire spectrum. No one was left untouched.

Many had no anchor and were uprooted with the hardships that came because of the virus. It was a change that nobody expected. We didn't *choose* this change. It was something that just happened, which is often the way change occurs. Instead of being deliberate in their actions, people just began reacting to the circumstances—myself included in the beginning. Some turned to control and began buying up as much as they could. A dear friend of mine has enough toilet paper to last her until Jesus comes back for us. I had to sit her down and have a toilet paper intervention.

On a more professional front, companies furloughed thousands. And homes were filled with both parents and children trying to work side by side on the same internet connection.

Some turned to conflict. I saw an actual fight break out in the grocery store over hand sanitizer. Everyone demanded a bailout. Politicians used social media to jab each other. And the media played the blame game. Too many of us failed to look at the bigger picture.

On the flip side, there were some who took a different approach and tried to see the greater picture. Some had faith that we would move through it quickly. Others assumed positive intent from perfect strangers. Some stopped listening to the media, which at times seemed to be spinning us out of control and creating fear, and created positive content instead. And some chose to serve where they could.

For example, Lindsey—a young woman I know, but never met (she's in my Sunday night Zoom LifeGroup)—chose to find ways to serve her apartment community in the Bronx. The neighbors in her apartment were elderly and she was concerned for them going out to get groceries. She doesn't have a lot of financial means, but put a note on her door that if anyone needed anything from the store, she would be happy to get it for them and leave it at their door, and she would cover the cost of the groceries.

Lindsey told us that it was her belief in the greater good that led her to do something like this. She also said it was out of her norm, as she is an introvert and doesn't necessarily interact with the other people who live in her building. Slowly, people started leaving her notes on small things they needed, and she joyfully filled the requests. Rather than worrying about the money, she focused on something bigger than herself—other people. It's the small gestures like this that help us lean into our spirituality.

Corporations also leaned into the greater good during the pandemic. Some corporate leaders took huge pay cuts or gave money out of their own pockets to help pay their employees' salaries. Others found ways they could cut costs so they wouldn't have to cut employees. While still, others found creative ways to keep their employees working so they wouldn't lose their jobs. Raytheon Technologies, my current employer, is an example of a company that got creative to help solve problems that stemmed from COVID.

The company comprises four independent businesses. Two are aerospace (Collins Aerospace and Pratt & Whitney), and two are defense (Raytheon Intelligence & Space and Raytheon Missiles & Defense). Obviously, as a result of the pandemic, the aerospace side of the house struggled while the defense side of the house boomed. As part of our efforts to remain viable, we had to reduce our workforce in the aerospace businesses by up to 30 percent in some cases. This happened through voluntary and involuntary separations—which was difficult.

In an effort to look beyond the "task" and focus on the employees, we decided to hold info sessions and virtual career fairs across the businesses. This is something that was unheard of prior to COVID. This means that employees displaced from aerospace were given the opportunity to learn about jobs and potential employment opportunities from the defense companies. It was a win-win for everyone involved. Throughout the entire process, everyone involved was committed to the greater good.

The above approaches were all spiritually based, meaning they were tied to something greater than ourselves. If we all approached the pandemic with this kind of mindfulness, we might have had a different response as a society.

Most people who have intentionally rooted themselves in spirituality and faith are kinder, more open-minded, and less reactive. They don't allow the world or their circumstances to dictate the kind of person they're going to be. This doesn't mean that they're moving through the situation with blinders on. They're fully aware of what's happening, but they're making a conscious choice on how to behave and what route to take. They see the bigger picture, and they've found their place in it. They've learned to trust the process.

Spirituality is being aware of the world around us and determining what we can do to be the good in it. Let me give you one more example. Our CFO and our Controller at Collins, both of whom I love working and partnering with, made difficult and personal decisions rooted in spiritualty—or the greater good for the function.

Neither were ready to retire and both had passion for jobs they did. They were well-regarded senior executives for the company. Yet both made the decision to retire early to make room for others who were ready for their roles and still had a lengthy career in front of them. When I talked to them about their decision, they were both in a peaceful place and expressed that their decision wasn't about them, it was about those who needed a place to go. Retiring early from a company has some personal implications tied to it and both chose to forego those for the bigger picture.

These remarkable individuals were fully aware of the world around them and what was happening in our company. They chose to root firmly in the good that they could do for others. I had tremendous respect for these two people prior to all of this and that goes unchanged. What has changed is how I view the choices we sometimes have to make when faced with really tough circumstances. The impact they left on me personally is profound.

They taught me that with our personal or corporate center-branch firmly rooted in spirituality, we're able to face negative circumstances with a more positive and hopeful approach.

THE VOID OF NOTHINGNESS

When we fail to get rooted in spirituality, we're left with what I call a void of nothingness. Just to be clear, this has nothing to do with the mystical void of nothingness. What I'm talking about is a literal void where nothing can grow effectively. This is how vital spirituality is to our root system. Why?

Because every other vital root we've discussed thus far will be nurtured when we nurture our spirituality root; love, relationship, trust, integrity, service, and joy will all be strengthened when we choose to root our centerbranch in spirituality. Spirituality encourages us to look outside of ourselves while still polishing our inner vessel. Spirituality also leads us to ask the important questions of where we came from, why we're here, where we're going, and how can we contribute to the world around us. These questions lead to self-reflection and discovery. And questions, self-reflection, and discovery can lead us to greater understanding and growth.

We've all experienced nothingness. It's empty, lonely, and dark. I once had a conversation with a CEO friend who told me that, as ironic as it sounds, the worst pain he's ever felt is feeling nothing. He went on to say that feeling nothing, or being void of having something to feel or believe in, is actually a painful place to be. It's a constant feeling that something's missing. I think that many of us can relate to that.

Many times, that pain comes because we have nothing greater to put our faith in, so the only thing we actually believe in is ourselves. While there is nothing wrong with having a strong belief in ourselves, the challenge tends to come when we think that everything is dependent on us. And when we fall short—which always happens (unless you are a narcissist), we look for something to distract us from our problems and something to fill the void. We may try to fill the void and numb the pain by self-medicating with alcohol, drugs, food, shopping, excessive exercising, or a million other addictions that can fill in the blank. Or we might choose to retreat to loneliness and self-isolation. All these things may bring short-term fixes, but never long-term happiness.

I call this distraction tactic "band-aiding" because of the nature of the problem. When we shop or vacation or do something to temporarily fill the void of nothingness or stop the pain, it's like we're applying a band-aid to the problem. It may help in the short-term, and it may even temporarily hide the problem. But the band-aid always falls off, and we're still left with the wound, or the void that we were trying to ignore.

In the end, it's our relationship and connection with something bigger that actually fills the void. Spirituality is learning that it's not all dependent on us, which instills a sense of hopefulness, especially in times of change. By remembering that there's always something greater than us, we're given the ability to hope that things will eventually work themselves out. Sometimes the reminder is gentle, and other times ambiguity and stress make it feel like a jerky roller coaster. Yet, in each instance, spirituality reminds us that every circumstance we face is exactly what we need for our own experience and growth.

DEFINING FAITH

Faith is vital when growing through change. We can have faith for the best version of who we are, faith in our company, faith in our country, or faith in humanity. Faith doesn't have to be a religious thing, but it can be for some of us. We can have faith in Buddha, the universe, God, or Jesus Christ. Faith is simply our ability to believe in something greater than us—to see beyond the right here and right now.

Faith allows us to take a step back and see an entire tapestry, instead of just the individual threads that we use to create it.

Because faith is seeing the bigger picture, rather than only what we're experiencing in the moment, it gives us a new perspective. With this newfound perspective, no matter what we choose to put our faith in, faith brings hope. And hope is our ability to recognize that there will always be greater things to come. This is why it's an essential mindset for managing change.

This doesn't mean that everything is going to be rainbows and butterflies. I have faith in something greater and I have hope that the difficult things I experience will be for my better good. I'm also cognizant that life is often difficult, complicated, and arduous work. I choose not to get bogged down in trying to control my way through it. I do my part by focusing on the small pieces that I can control—which are actually very little (my health, my mindset, my responses)—and I stop there. We can all benefit from making that same kind of choice.

That's where our faith leads to hope and we choose to trust that it's all going to work itself out. We can do our part, while no longer trying to control every single aspect of our life. We no longer fall victim to life's circumstances because we trust in the process. That's what faith can provide for us—peace of mind even in times of trouble.

OUR NEED FOR LIGHT

We've all experienced nothingness. It's empty, lonely, and dark. When I think of it, I think of entering a room that is pitch dark. When you first walk in, you can't see a thing. But after a few minutes of being in the dark, you can start to make out shapes. It's not perfect vision, and there's no detail, but you get used to it.

This is a perfect analogy of how people live in that place of nothingness. Either the light goes out, or the light was never there to begin with, and we just slowly adjust to the darkness. It becomes our new way of living. We stop looking for the big picture since we can only see what's right in front of us. Because of this, we slowly adjust our behaviors and our mindset, basing them solely on what we can see.

Gradually, over time, this becomes our new norm. And pretty soon, emptiness and nothingness become our full-time companion. Because we live in the dark, we lead in the dark. And everyone who joins our organization becomes accustomed to working in a place void of light. It impedes our progress and the progress of others.

Many of us live in a place of nothingness, and we're not even aware of it. We have no idea that the lights have been turned out and we're living and leading in the dark. I lived this way for many years.

When the light was finally turned on for me, I was blinded in the beginning because I had been operating in the dark for so long. But gradually, I became accustomed to it. As I looked around with the light on, I was able to see so many things that were probably always there, but I never saw before.

For example, as simple as this sounds, I started to notice the vibrancy of color and sound. I remember sitting in a car at a Starbucks somewhere in Texas, and it was as if I had new eyes and new ears. I sat there watching people walk in and out, noticing the colors of the clothes they were wearing, recognizing the lush greenery of the trees around me, and hearing the birds chirping—which suddenly sounded like surround sound. It was somewhat overwhelming to me because those little things had always been there, but I didn't see or hear them because of the blinders and earmuffs of darkness that shrouded me.

I also started to see how differently other people's perspectives were from mine. Maybe I didn't care before—maybe since I was in the dark, I didn't ask. I don't know the reason, but what I do know is that I started asking more questions and genuinely seeking answers. I found that I was surrounded by a group of people who had so much good to offer me and were major contributors to my well-being. Because of this, I was more open to them. When in the dark, I felt like I was going it alone. I didn't know other people were there to help—I couldn't see them. It's incredible to me how different our perspective can be by simply turning the light on.

OUR INNER STRENGTH

Spirituality is that inner light that sheds understanding on the outside world. It's inner security when our external security is threatened. When our entire world is in chaos, it gives us the ability to calm the storm within. Let me give you a very real and very visual example of this.

I live in Florida, and when we're in the middle of hurricane season, it's not uncommon for summer storms. One night we had a ferocious storm blow in from out of nowhere. I was sitting in my all-glass sunroom (my literal happy place) when it started to storm. I was interested in the sudden change in light, so I stood up and walked to the middle of the room to get a better view of the storm.

The emerald green of expansive golf course and the sapphire blue of the sky were gone in an instant and replaced by dark greys and winds so fierce that I watched the palm trees bend horizontally. I made me wonder if we were going to have a tornado. It was hailing, thundering, and howling on all sides of me in my sunroom—yet I had a feeling of complete stillness and peace within me. I knew this would pass, and I would be just fine.

Although part of my brain told me to run and get in the bathtub (Tornado 101), the other part of my brain told me that this too, shall pass. For me, this was a completely spiritual experience. It was almost as if I were looking down at myself in the eye of the emotional storm I am living today with COVID, my job, and a transition to my own company—and having a knowing that it would all be just fine as long as I held on to my faith.

Spirituality makes it possible for us to see the bigger picture. This, in turn, allows us to readjust what we're seeing by providing a better perspective. And when we readjust what we're seeing and experiencing, we can readjust how we navigate through life, through change, and through every interaction.

As leaders, it's our responsibility to turn the lights on for people. We can do that in a variety of different ways. We can challenge people in coaching conversations to think differently. We can invite them to see situations from a new paradigm. We can simply show them kindness and compassion. We can instill mindfulness and meditation in the workplace. Or we can make sure there is always a whole-self integration. In many ways, spirituality is helping people feel something from the inside out. It's lighting a spark inside of them and giving them a reason to live in the light.

Life is much more vibrant when we choose to live in the light. Not only can we see the bigger picture for our own life and company, but we can start to really make a difference in the world.

DISCOVERING MY OWN LIGHT

When I was living in that space of nothingness, it was Jesus that turned the light on for me. Now I know this is a book about change, but I wouldn't be true to myself if I didn't share where my greatest change in life came from. And although spirituality may look different for you, for me, it looks like Jesus. Meeting Jesus was the first time I felt full and loved. He changed the way I see the world, which carries over to how I work and live.

If you have an aversion to talking about religion, and more especially, Jesus, feel free to skip this section. But if you're interested in how the light came on for me, read on.

Jesus was a real man who taught real people how to live their lives better. That alone should make his life a subject of study. But for me, my relationship with Jesus is so much more. Once I realized I could actually have a relationship and connection with him, my life drastically changed for the better. My relationship with Jesus helped me to realize that there really was something greater than myself to believe in.

I didn't come to my belief in Jesus lightly. I was never a religious child, and my family certainly wasn't a religious family. I remember when I was in middle school, I purchased a cross for my mom with the points I earned from having good grades. It was a Christmas gift for her. At the time, I had no idea what it symbolized. I didn't know who Jesus was. But there was a kind of beauty in that cross, and I was drawn to buying it. I realized even then that Jesus was trying to get my attention.

I was so excited and so proud to give my mom her Christmas gift that year. But as soon as she opened it, she seemed confused and maybe even offended by the gift. She asked me why I would buy such a gift and asked if I thought she needed it. I felt terrible afterward. I have no idea what my mother did with that necklace, and we never brought it up again. This experience, and countless others, solidified to me that we definitely lived in that space of nothingness as a family. As a side note, I am happy to report that years later, I bought my mother another cross necklace (a matching one to one of mine) and she wears it all the time. I planted the seed as a child and her faith has grown and actually rooted in her, just as it's rooted in me. It's important to remember that spirituality is always growing and changing.

When I was a child, my spirituality was just a seed. As meaningful spiritual experiences came, that seed grew. When I was in high school, I went through a lot of personal trauma. I remember thinking that there had to be something bigger or better than what I was experiencing. I was a straight-A student with good attendance, but I didn't feel like I had a purpose. I became a cutter hoping people would notice; they never did.

One day as I was cutting, I had a simple yet profound thought, as if someone else was speaking the words to me, "Stop it. You are loved." These simple five words pierced my heart, and I never cut myself again. As I look back, I know that was God speaking to my mind and my heart.

Because love never flowed freely from my family, I constantly struggled with a feeling of emptiness. I was taken care of, but I never felt loved. I'm certain that my parents loved me; I just don't think they were equipped with how to show it. I took this void into adulthood and every relationship I had, including my marriage. My husband's family was the first family I had ever experienced that was close-knit and had a relationship with Jesus. My husband's mother encouraged us to find a church ourselves, so we went church shopping.

We tried on a few churches. Some were interesting, some were a flat out "uh, nope" and some were just ok. The moment I walked into Victory Church in Philadelphia, I had an over-whelming sense of warmth. It was as if someone had wrapped me up with an electric blanket and was holding me tight. It was overwhelming at first because I didn't know what I didn't know. People would sing loudly and praise boldly, and all I could do was watch them.

Over the course of time, I went from arms at my side and singing under my breath to both hands raised, praising Jesus for everything. The more I learned how awesome Jesus was, the more grateful I became to my husband's parents. They changed my life, and I am forever grateful for the seed they planted in me. Although my marriage ended because of the trauma of multiple miscarriages, emotional abuse, and a battle for control, I would never change what I was given because of it. I felt loved, and I was able to learn how to give love in return.

SPIRITUALITY PROVIDES PURPOSE

My entire life leading up to that point, I never had faith. I had curiosity but no foundation. Like a broken vessel, I was cracked due to my childhood and marriage trauma. When I met Jesus, it was as if he poured his light in me and filled all my cracks with gold. The difference was very noticeable to those around me, in both my personal and professional life.

When people asked me what's caused such a profound difference in my life, my answer was, and still is, simple. "It's Jesus. We're dating. He's really cool." In full disclosure, I have a tendency to be sarcastic and sometimes say things for shock value.

So, while my "It's Jesus!" response was a very true statement, it did raise some eyebrows—which I was fine with.

When I found Jesus, I was giddy and wanted to tell everyone. It was like Jesus was my new boyfriend. I couldn't help but tell people about him. I'm not talking about the Bible-bashing, "you better repent!" kind of conversation. That's not who I am. I'm talking about the "Jesus has been so good to me, wanna hear about it?" kind of conversation. I was bursting to tell people all the good things Jesus had done for me, and I still carry that feeling today.

I may not actually be dating Jesus, but he has certainly turned the light on in me. And that inner light is showing up on the outside. I'm a completely different person. I'm happier, and that happiness flows to other people, especially in my work life. That happiness has changed me and changed my environment. I'm more mindful of people and where they're coming from. I'm more willing to give compliments and encouragement. I've stopped taking myself so seriously and I've learned to share the load. I trust more because I know that Jesus trusts me—he's always got my back. And most of all, I've found my sense of purpose.

That's what inner light can do.

FINDING YOUR OWN INNER LIGHT

If we, as leaders, turned our inner light on, imagine what kind of effect we could have in our own homes and workplaces. When we turn our own light on, it inspires others to do the same. And that inner light is one of the greatest commodities we can have to manage both personal and corporate change successfully.

Through my spirituality and faith, I believe in something greater than myself. I'm by no means perfect. I consider myself very flawed and I still make poor decisions and experience moments of frustration. But I know I have the grace from God that allows me to try again and improve. I'm not judged, just loved. This is now the same kind of grace I try to extend to my own employees. God doesn't expect me to be perfect, and I shouldn't expect that of others. I do have high expectations and expect good work to be done, but I don't expect perfection.

I believe that there is something better for all of us. And I have hope that one day we find it. For many of you, your inner light may not come from Jesus. Wherever it comes from, that same feeling, connection, relationship, and purpose that I felt with him is what we need to find and root ourselves in. It's what we need for our company and for the people we employ. If nothing else, it's faith in humanity and the good that we can do when we choose to focus on the bigger picture—those things that are greater than us all.

I realize that there are very few places where we can talk about Jesus in the workplace. We don't have to talk about Jesus to become more like him, or Mother Teresa, or Muhammad, or Buddha, or Florence Nightingale, or Sir Francis of Assisi. These people, and many others, are perfect examples of how we can spend our lives inspiring others to become the best version of themselves. These men and women recognized that there was something greater and they saw the bigger picture.

Faith and spirituality are so much more than religion. It's mindfulness. It's recognizing our humanity and being mindful of the conscious choices we're making. It's about choosing to follow the examples of good men and women who came before us—people who devoted their lives to serve and bless others and to be the good in the world. It's about you and me determining what kind of person we're going to be and what kind of company we want to be a part of.

Spirituality is looking beyond the here and now and seeing a purpose for the circumstances we find ourselves in, and inspiring others to see that purpose too. It's finding hope in the adventures that await us on the other side of the ocean. And it's putting our faith in those invisible things that will one day take us places where we cannot go on our own.

PUTTING IT INTO PRACTICE

1. Take ten to thirty minutes a day and practice mindfulness. Do a Google search for hundreds of ways to practice. My favorite, right now, is Shirzad Chamine—which is actually on Positive Intelligence more than mindfulness.

2. Identify something in your life that is bigger than you. How can shifting your perspective from self to that bigger "thing" help you? How will this impact your thoughts and actions?

3. Determine one or two actions that you can take to help someone out of a space of nothingness.

4. Determine a time when you felt like you were living in a void of nothingness? Are you living in that space now? What occurred to get you to this place? What did you do, or what can you do, to find your way out of it?

5. What can you put your faith in that is outside of your control/purview? How will doing this help you to move out of nothingness?

6. What is it about your company's greater mission or vision that you can connect with? Write down ten ways your role or your actions impact that greater mission.

7. Read or listen to good uplifting books that bring you clarity.

8. Spend thirty minutes in nature, either walking or sitting, and recognize the beauty around you.

9. Identify ways where you are filling your void of nothingness that is only bringing you short-term happiness. For me, it was shopping all the time. Others may overeat or even overexercise. What is it that you use to fill your nothingness? How can you replace those short-term fixes with true long-term happiness?

10. If you don't believe in God, consider the possibilities. Maybe go church-shopping and find a place where you feel that you belong.

CHAPTER 10

PROGRESS VS. PERFECTION

"You will find that it is necessary to let things go; simply for the reason that they are heavy."

—C. JoyBell C.

When I worked for Bridgestone, I had the privilege of running our global leadership development function. This function was an internal service provider for all things learning, development, and talent management. The CFO was one of the leaders who had direct access to our services. One of my employees was a dedicated resource for our CFO and his finance function. This employee had full responsibility for the talent development and talent moves that happened in Finance. Because this employee and I were both new in the position, we partnered very closely in the beginning.

One of our first projects together was to create a talent review that was specifically designed for the finance organization. I struggled a lot with this project because I saw the CFO as a big internal client with a high-ranking job and I wasn't completely confident in myself or my ability to deliver what he wanted. It was a new job in a new role, and I wanted more than anything to make the best first impression possible. I also wanted to make sure I was delivering, not just what I promised, but exactly what he expected.

I was not at all secure in my role, so rather than being a consultative partner and trying to help him figure out his challenges, I just took the order and did what he said without really understanding what he needed. Because of this, I was stuck in a cycle of perfection.

·

THE PROBLEM WITH PERFECTION

Because my expectations on myself are much higher than anyone else's—I became stuck. And when I say I got stuck, what really happened is that I was in a complete downward spiral. I would do a part of the project, tell myself it wasn't perfect, go back and redo the project, only to once again realize it wasn't perfect. I ended up spinning out and going nowhere. I was like a cat chasing its tail—always running, but getting nowhere.

The project became significantly delayed, and I found myself right smack dab in a status meeting with the CFO. The meeting began with him questioning me on what was happening to cause such a significant delay.

In my mind, it was perfectly fine to be delayed because the project wasn't perfect yet. Once we began our conversation, I realized this was definitely not the case. It wasn't fine at all. He was very frustrated with me because the project was important to him, and I was missing deadlines.

"What is it that's holding you up?" he asked.

I explained to him what I had done with the project and where I wanted to go with it. And then I said, "It's just not where it needs to be. It's not perfect yet."

He stopped me right there. "Nothing is ever perfect, Stacy," he said. "Good is good."

He then motioned for me to sit down. We usually had "stand-up" meetings, so I knew when he told me to sit down, it wasn't going to be good. He then had a very serious mentoring conversation with me. He told me that trying to be perfect and diligent in everything—all of the time—is what derails careers. He gave me a few not-so-lovely examples of careers being derailed, catching on fire, and/or imploding because of perfectionism. I was not expecting this conversation and it left me shaky.

I honestly had never thought of perfection in that way before.

Up to that point in my life, I never saw perfection as a career derailer; I saw it as a career accelerator. Because of this, perfection is what I strived for in everything I was a part of. It was my go-to way of being. I wanted everything perfect. And I worked myself ragged to make it happen.

The CFO reminded me that no one would know whether it was perfect or good, except for me. And that the most important thing we can do is keep our commitments, especially when our deliverables are necessary to move an organization forward into its next phase of growth. He also taught me that it doesn't really matter if it's perfect or good, because good is still good and will move the company forward. And as we move forward, we can improve the process, making it better and better.

"That's progress," he said, "Progress is what we're looking for—not perfection."

To be honest, I was a little frustrated with myself. I felt let down, and that I had let him down. I was worried about my reputation and how people perceived me.

As I got up to walk away, his final words really hit me, "This is a good learning lesson for you, Stacy. Because at the end of the day, the more these types of things happen, the less people will be able to rely on you. Good is good—the main objective is to deliver. Don't let perfection get in the way of progress, or people will stop believing in you."

This was one of the hardest messages for me to hear, but it absolutely changed how I approached things in both my personal and professional life. And his counsel is the basis of this chapter.

My goal was always perfection, but my own ideas of what perfection looked like were getting in the way of actually moving forward.

PERFECTION IS LIKE A UNICORN

The hard truth is that my ideas of perfection were wrong. Nobody knows what perfection looks like. We may think we know, but there are no parameters and no absolutes. You can't define it. The idea of perfection is completely based on the thoughts and opinions of the beholder. My perfect may look very different than your perfect. My CEO's perfect may look wildly different than my neighbor's perfect. And even our ideas of perfection aren't perfect. This makes our pursuit of perfection an unattainable goal.

If we make perfection our quest, we may as well try to catch a unicorn at the same time. We know unicorns are mythical creatures and that the possibility of catching one is at an absolute zero. Unless, of course, you're playing a virtual game in a virtual world—then your chances may be pretty good. But we don't live in a virtual world. We live in the here and now. In the real world, unicorns don't exist, and neither does perfection.

Yet we're constantly searching for it and expecting others to have it as well. We're setting ourselves up for failure and disappointment every time.

From a personal perspective, we use social media to compare our house, our job, and our life, to our neighbors' house, or job, or life. Through these very superficial comparisons, we mistakenly believe that everyone else is living a perfect life. This is a ridiculous way to live our lives—and I do mean ridiculous. This unhealthy comparison just drives us to want to be more perfect as we try to chase some unattainable make-believe version of what we believe our life should be. This perfection mindset severely hinders us from living the life we have.

I always thought perfection was the end game. It was my objective in everything that I set out to accomplish. I wanted to be the perfect person with the perfect house and the perfect job. I even wanted to be the perfect wife, the perfect friend, and the perfect employee. But it never occurred to me that my objective was what was holding me back. It was crushing me and tearing me apart from the inside out. With an objective of perfection, I was guaranteed to fail. And it was my own idea of failure that was slowly killing me.

FAILURE BRINGS GROWTH

If you're like I was and believe in the false idea of perfection, I have two words for you—STOP IT! Stop it right now. The perfection mindset is a dangerous mindset. If you continue down that destructive path, it can eat you up and destroy you. That may seem a little rash to say, but believe me, it's true. Don't buy into what the world and your own mind is selling you. There's a better and more attainable way to go about it—that path is progress.

In order to embrace progress, we have to let go of the dangerous belief that if it's not perfect, it's a failure. Many of us mistakenly believe that perfection is the goal and failure should be avoided at all costs. The truth is completely opposite of that. Perfection stalls our progress while failure propels us forward. We should embrace failure as it is another catalyst for growth. This was a mindset I had to nurture for myself.

Some of the biggest and boldest innovations in history have happened because someone failed the first time. Scientists and inventors weren't looking for perfection, they were looking for a functional prototype. And with each failed iteration, their work became better and better. That's progress. And progress is what we're looking for. There's a heck of a lot of failure that had to happen in order for us to progress to where we are as a society.

We've somehow forgotten that. In the pace of today's society, with technology and information at our fingertips, and a constant connection to the internet, we've forgotten how progress works. Our pace and expectations are even greater than before.

We want things done quicker, better, and bolder. And failure is unacceptable.

As leaders, we need to recognize that there are going to be multiple failures in the process. And multiple times doing the same thing in order to get it incrementally better. We need to adjust our understanding of what failure looks like. Failure isn't actually failure if it's moving us forward.

Let me give you another example. While at Carrier, I was tasked by the chief human resources officer (CHRO) to develop an HR development program for a select group of high-potential HR professionals. My muscle memory immediately kicked in and I wanted the program to be perfect. It was my first big project and the CHRO had very high expectations. Thankfully, that moment was fleeting, and I snapped back into the reality of "good."

At the time, Carrier didn't have any formal development programs for the HR population—or for any population. So I took this opportunity to lay the groundwork for a suite of standardized, multitier, career-progressive development offerings. I put together an eight-month, high-potential development program that targeted mid-career individuals who had executive potential. There was a tremendous amount of visibility with this program, and every day I battled the need to put progress in front of perfection.

We kicked the program off with a livestream event where I

moderated a sixty-minute panel interview with several of our senior executives in HR. It was good—very good, actually. It was not perfect. Over the next eight months, we ran the program virtually as I had designed it. Some of it was good and it worked well. Some of it was not good, and it didn't really work at all. There was even one portion that was a bit of a failure.

Even still, no one seemed to notice because we had made such progress with the program itself. Over time, the program went through iterations and morphed into an even better program. That proof of concept program did indeed lay the groundwork for additional amazing development offerings called *Talent Possible*. I am proud of that not perfect, yet good program. I am even more proud of the progress I made by not giving into perfectionism and the progress that Carrier made by moving through some of the failures of that program with ease. I have since moved on, and the new team is doing even more amazing things with *Talent Possible*. What I saw as a failure was simply our good program moving forward.

In light of this, we should be asking ourselves and others, "How did you fail today?" We need to celebrate our failures. And we have to be willing to fail in order to actually progress. When our focus is on progress, we can better recognize that any progress is better than no progress.

When we let go of the idea of, "if it's not perfect, it's a failure," we'll more fully recognize that it's not just one or the other.

Life isn't black and white. There's a whole spectrum of good in there that we're missing when our entire focus is on perfection.

GOOD IS GOOD

Good isn't a bad word, and it isn't a swear word—although many of us see it that way. The actual dictionary definition says that good is a desirable thing. When our focus is on perfection, we forget that good is actually still really good. It's desirable. Yet we often use it in a derogatory way, "It's good, but it's not perfect." This makes it sound as if it's "less than" in value when compared to perfection. We need to acknowledge our progress and stop negating the good work we've already done.

Let me give you a personal example from my own life. I've been on a journey to get healthier. For the past four months, I've gone to the gym pretty consistently. I've got out of bed early, and I've been mindful of what I eat. I'm actually losing weight, but my whole purpose in doing this is to simply get healthier.

Now, a former version of myself would have had things so well planned out that I would have already been at my goal by now, and everything would have been implemented perfectly. It would have been so regimented that at the end of reaching my goal, when I went back to my "normal life," I would not have been able to transition back. And after a few months, I would have ended up right back where I started.

But this time, I'm Stacy 2.0. I'm giving myself a break from perfection, and I'm actually making progress. There are weeks where I lose two pounds. There are weeks where I stay the same. And there are weeks where I gain a pound because I enjoy pizza and wine with a friend. But after I eat that pizza and drink that wine with a friend, I get up the next morning and go to the gym—and that's progress. When I look back to where I was four months ago, I'm happy with the results. I've made progress, and progress is good.

Moving through change is often a matter of focus and perspective. If my focus is on how perfect I eat each day, or how soon I'll reach my goal, I miss seeing the progress that comes inch by inch, pound by pound, and day by day.

By rooting our centerbranch in progress, we're able to see the good that's taking us places. Recognizing that progress helps us to let go of the impossible expectations that come from our idea of perfection.

GET RID OF IMPOSSIBLE EXPECTATIONS

I'm a recovering "high-expectationist." I know I just made up that word, but there's no other word for it, so work with me. What I mean by a high-expectationist is that my expectations on my staff and the people around me used to be ridiculously high. The expectations I had on myself were even higher—I'm talking unrealistically high.

I would get frustrated when my employees didn't live up to my expectations. When I was living as a high-expectationist, I couldn't understand why people were always disappointing me. I couldn't figure out why their work was always below my expectations. And many times, I would just redo the work myself. I fully admit, looking back, that I was seriously crazy. I'm surprised my employees stayed in that kind of environment. During a performance review, I even had an employee tell me once that she quit trying to submit good work because she knew I would just redo it to my own expectations anyway. She said that she used to go above and beyond to do work that she was really proud of, but it was never good enough for me, so she stopped trying and was less stressed out. This was really hard to hear, so I asked her what I could do differently.

Her response was so simple: "Acknowledge my good work and don't change it unless it is just wrong. And if it is wrong, let me know so I can fix it."

This courageous employee was the only one who had the courage to tell me my expectations were unreasonable. And I am actually very grateful she did. Don't get me wrong, it sucked hearing it, but it was something I needed to hear.

We're all human. My drive for perfection compelled me to continually place unfair expectations on myself and everyone around me. I expected superhuman abilities perfectly executed. But when I uprooted that perfection root and rooted my centerbranch in progress instead, I discovered that the greatest gift I could give to myself and others was grace. My employees have always been good employees, and the more I let go of perfection, the more I was able to see how truly wonderful they were.

As leaders, we're constantly searching for the perfect candidate. But we fail to recognize the good employees all around us. There are well-placed, solid, well-round people who are doing their very best. They're not perfect, but they're hard workers. Their good is doing good things for the company.

By letting go of the perfection mindset, we're able to see what perfection blinded us from. There's no such thing as a perfect person, so we're never going to find the perfect employee. From a performance standpoint, unless you're NASA, only 5-7 percent of your population will be in the high performing, high potential box. The bulk of your population will be average performance and average potential. In the nine-box grid, the middle box is still labeled "good." These are the people who you need to get the daily work done to keep the company engine moving.

Good employees are important and essential. I've learned not to discount the good employees to hold out for the perfect candidates. Because the perfect employee is just like that mythical unicorn—they don't exist.

Once I stopped expecting perfect employees, I saw the good

work they were doing and the progression we were making together. Focusing on progress has changed the way I work. It's brought less disappointment because I no longer have impossible expectations for myself or for others. And as a bonus, my employees actually like working with me.

Remember—good is good and done is better than perfect. When a project is good and done, progress happens, and change is more easily managed.

PROGRESS OVER PERFECTION

I've saved the value of progress until the last chapter because after all is said and done, change is our ability to progress. Whether we want to admit it or not, we're always in a constant state of change. Every time we make a choice, we're potentially changing the direction that we're going. When those changes present themselves, if we get caught up in the expectation of perfection, we can severely stunt our growth and the growth of our company.

For high achievers, like myself, our focus on perfection can become a downward spiral in our ability to grow and progress through change. If something isn't perfect, we tend to try even harder to force perfection. We fixate on what's missing in our relationships, our home, our workplace, or even in ourselves. This will hurt us in the end. We'll stay stuck and unable to move forward. And we'll severely damage our relationships.

We've got to learn how to lean into change without worrying about the perfection side of things. Change is hard enough without placing those unrealistic expectations on ourselves and those around us.

Change is messy. It's uncomfortable, and it's vulnerable. It's getting down in the dirt and digging up roots that no longer serve us. It can be exhausting. Whether it's personal change or corporate change, it's hard work. But any work that you do is moving you forward.

Change is also helping make a better landscape for ourselves and our company. Instead of a patch of weeds, we'll have a garden of possibilities.

On the other side of the change, we'll look back to where we started from and see just how transformational our progress has become. We'll realize that each failure was a launching pad for greater success. And above all, we'll recognize that perfection was never even required.

PROGRESS AND CHANGE

One of the worst things we can do to set ourselves up for failure is to believe that changes will happen overnight. We may have this unrealistic expectation that when change happens, everything will be perfect on the other side of it. Everyone will know their new responsibilities, and everyone will be happy with the changes. We'll immediately see exponential growth, and life will just be better. Expecting perfection right out of the starting gate is not a healthy strategy for anyone. Instead, we need to acknowledge and respect that any progress takes time.

If change were easy and perfection could be attained right out of the starting gate, there wouldn't be thousands of books and podcasts and people speaking on change management. It would be as simple as brushing our teeth at night. But change is a process. And sometimes that process is long and complicated. As humans, we have to think through the challenges, process the emotions, and make several important choices along the way.

Change is a step by step process of knowledge, reflection, acceptance, and growth. It's a different process for each of us as we look at the change through our own paradigm.

Progress means accepting that there will be aspects of life that will be different on the other side of that change. It's easy to stay in the mindset of, "Well this is how I've always done it." But this way of thinking keeps us stuck in the past. And when we get stuck in the way things used to be, we stop growing, both individually and as a company.

Growing through change means being okay with different. Different doesn't have to be a bad thing. Different is just different. It has the potential to be good, exciting, and refreshing.

Different can bring us new opportunities and relationships. It also has the potential to bring us good things that we never even knew we wanted.

Of course, different can also be sad, and it's perfectly fine to grieve for what was left behind. But we can't get stuck looking behind us. We have to keep progressing—and progress will always mean change. Things have to be different in order to grow. If a seed stayed a seed forever, there would never be roots. There would never be trees, and there would never be the magnificent fruit that comes from a bountiful harvest.

Like seeds, our growth will also require us to change.

GET ROOTED IN PROGRESS

Remember, life isn't about perfection; it's about progress. It doesn't matter how you grow, as long as you grow. Good roots make good trees. Good roots also make good people.

History has shown us that nothing stays the same. If we were to look back over the hundreds and thousands of years before us, the world has changed significantly. And it keeps changing. The greatest thing we can do for ourselves is to get rooted and learn to change with the change. That's essentially what progress is all about.

With the events of COVID-19, it's easy to see how quickly

change can come upon us. It was a stark reminder that change is inevitable. And the only way to stay strong when those winds blow is to find our centerbranch, nurture our good roots, and allow the change to come.

PUTTING IT INTO PRACTICE

1. Think of one area in your life where perfection has held you back. What would you do differently if given the opportunity? If possible, do something to move forward in that area.

2. Think of a thirty-day goal. Create a thirty-day calendar with small steps of daily progress toward that goal. On days you don't make progress, put a smiley face signaling that you aren't looking for perfection. Pro tip: the intent here is to *not* be perfect in your actions...and to extend yourself some grace for not being perfect. Perfectly completing a thirty-day challenge is literally the opposite of this exercise.

3. Make a daily list of all the items that you *made progress on, started, accomplished, etc.* By the end of the week, you may not have perfectly completed everything, but you'll have a long list of progresses!

4. Write down five statements that you might normally make to yourself if you are stuck in a perfection spiral. Now re-write those statements with the focus on what you *have done* instead of what you *haven't done.* Then, say them out loud. Maybe even record them on your phone and listen to them on playback. It can be very impactful to hear your own voice say good things about yourself—something we don't do often.

5. Make a list of five recent failures. Now cross out the word failure and re-write *Learning Experiences.* Then write all the lessons you learned from those five experiences. This helps us shift our mindset from perfection/failure to progress/learning.

6. If you're a perfectionist, make it a point to stop projecting your personal expectations on other people. Remind yourself that it's not about perfection, it's about their progress and growth. If you feel someone has not met your expectations, don't share your frustrations. Give them a compliment on what they have done right instead.

7. Find an accountability partner or trio who can help give you encouragement and hold you accountable to your goals. Remember, it's not about doing things perfectly, it's simply about progressing.

8. Create your own personal mantra around progress versus perfection

and put it on a sticky note where you can see it and repeat it daily.

9. Create a vision board of your goals and hang it up as a reminder of how you're trying to progress. Keep a list of all the things you have accomplished to show your progression.

10. Picture yourself ten years ago. Make a list of what's changed about you and your situation now. Picture yourself ten years from now. Where do you want to be? Make a list of the things you need to do to get you to where you want to go. Remember that progress takes time.

CONCLUSION

John Maxwell once wrote: "Change is inevitable. Growth is optional."

This quote perfectly sums up my message to you. Change is inevitable in our lives. We know that, especially after the events of COVID-19. Those moments may come quickly, and they may be completely unexpected. It's the choices we make in those moments that will define who we are and determine where we're headed.

WHAT WILL YOU CHOOSE?

Change may be inevitable, but growth is our choice. We have to choose to lean into it and to take those steps toward change, instead of running from it. That is the only way growth is going to happen. Change equals growth only if we choose to grow. However, growth will always mean change.

Abraham Maslow said: "In any given moment we have two options: to step forward into growth or step back into safety."

If we're not open to change, we cannot grow. We can mourn what we've lost and do all we can to step back into what's comfortable and safe. Or we can step forward into the unknown and experience the growth that is sure to come. Growth is progress and although it's uncomfortable, it will also bring greater success.

CHOOSE A VALUES-DRIVEN LIFE

One of the greatest examples of growth is the growth of a tree. There are trees that are thousands of years old and have only survived because they have good roots that run deep.

Just like good roots make good trees, the things that we root ourselves in will determine our own growth, especially when facing change.

If we're rooted in unhealthy ideas, these ideas cannot sustain us. They're damaging to our overall root system and are often based on self-centered practices. When the storms come, our roots will be too shallow to save us.

By rooting ourselves in good values and practicing values-driven leadership, we can grow our roots deep. These roots become an anchor, giving us something to hold onto when difficult changes come. Rooting ourselves in universal values will strengthen our entire root system.

By rooting yourself in the eight universal values covered in this book, you'll have the strength to weather the storms of change that come into your life. Together, these values can create a healthy root system that will survive and thrive any challenge that you're faced with and keep you from slipping back into those unhealthy ideas and actions that can derail you.

GROW HEALTHY ROOTS

As you choose to nurture **love** and let go of conflict, you'll gain a greater appreciation for yourself and those around you. By seeing others through a lens of love and respect, you can accentuate the good and create a positive atmosphere where ideas can be shared, and growth can happen.

By choosing to nurture **relationships, you** will strengthen your own ability to get through challenging transitions. It provides connection and collaboration, especially in the workplace. In an environment where relationships are valued, everyone feels important and needed. In this type of environment, disengagement rarely happens.

Nurturing **trust** will enable you to let go of control. Trusting the process gives you peace of mind that everything that happens will be for your good. Trusting the people around you will strengthen your relationships and allow for greater connection.

By choosing **integrity** over dishonesty, you become someone who can be trusted. Transparency and communication are key to moving through change effectively, especially when transitioning a company where many people are involved and will be affected by the change. Rooting yourself in integrity will keep everyone moving through the change with less conflict and more genuine trust for the process.

As you nurture **service**, not only will you strengthen relationships, but you'll set the example of what a good leader should do. A leader is someone who makes a difference in the lives of others. It doesn't require a title, just a desire to help others. We can all be servant leaders if we choose to be. And if we make that choice, we can help ourselves and others move through change more effectively.

Nurturing **joy** will help us to overcome complacency by enabling us to find our passion. Finding our own passion can inspire us to help develop the passion of others. By doing what we love to do, and finding the joy in every situation, we can use that same attitude to move through change. Once joy is a habit, it becomes a natural way of life, even in the hardest of times. Joy doesn't come from things. Joy is developed from the inside out.

Making the choice to nurture **spirituality** in your life will help you to remember that there's always something greater out there. By developing faith, whether that faith is in God or humanity, we can recognize that we're not alone. Spirituality brings an inner light that fills our own void of nothingness.

By choosing to nurture **progress** over perfection, we can let go of those unrealistic expectations we have for ourselves and others. We can courageously put one foot in front of the other and remember that nobody's perfect. Perfection may be impossible, but progress is exactly what we need to grow.

Nurturing these eight roots will provide a strong and deep root system that will keep you growing and thriving throughout your life. It's the exact root system I've used to move through count-less changes in my life. And with these exact roots, I've always come out the other side of those changes a better version of myself.

GET CONNECTED

When I think back to the Aspen tree, I'm reminded how every-thing is connected. Even though it looks like individual trees in the forest, every single tree is intertwined. Underneath that beautiful forest of Aspens, the roots and its massive glory are all part of the greater whole.

When all eight of these roots are nurtured, they will inter-twine and run deep. They all work together to ultimately keep you standing in a storm. The more of them you nurture, the stronger your roots will be, both individually and collectively. Relationships are strengthened through love; integrity influences trust; service increases joy. You can also say that trust improves relationships, you'll find joy in integrity, and greater love is developed through service. Every nourished root will strengthen and nourish all others. The connections can go on and on.

As people, we are also all connected. Our personal root system will ultimately touch the individual root systems of those around us. And those roots will touch a corporation's root system, which will reach out across the world. When we make it a priority to get rooted, our roots will ultimately strengthen everyone else around us.

CHOOSE CHANGE

In the end, when change comes, I hope you choose it. I hope you choose to grow and to develop strong roots that run deep. I hope that you take the questions in this book and apply them to your life again and again.

Above all, I hope you choose to get rooted in the values that matter.

Change is going to come, and it doesn't have to be a bad thing. When you're faced with change, I hope you envision yourself as a tree and remember that a tree has to change to grow. A tiny seed has a magnificent oak tree within its shell. But in order for that seed to reach its potential, it has to grow and change. If it stayed the same, it would only ever be a seed.

You and I are much like the tree. We have magnificent potential within us. But if we become too comfortable with who we currently are, we'll never know the magnitude of what we can become.

Choose change, embrace growth, and get rooted!

ACKNOWLEDGMENTS

To my family—I love you all very much. Thank you for all the life lessons—the good, the bad, and the tuna-noodle casserole. Most importantly, thank you for putting up with me when I wasn't rooted in the right things. I wouldn't be the person I am today without your love, support, and mockery.

To every single one of my friends who encouraged me along the way—Thank you so much! Your support means the world to me. To my friends who made fun of me along the way—just wait until the next book.

To my professional colleagues who inspired the stories in the book and contributed to who I am as a leader and person—I appreciate you. I value the servant leaders, the tough bosses, the hard lessons, the growth opportunities, the failures and successes, and the true work friends I've made along the way.

To the Sisters-in-Script review committee—Thank you so much for the honor of receiving your grant! I am so appreciative of the time you took to review my project, read my words, and offer such wonderful feedback.

To the Scribe team—WOW! WOW! WOW! Thank you to every single person who contributed to making this process so amazing. It is legitimately a dream come true and without all of you, it would have never happened. A very special thanks to Maggie and Tiffany.

Maggie—it was no accident that I was paired with you! From our first conversation, I knew we had a unique connection and I am so thankful that you played a part in my journey.

Tiffany—I cannot put to words how much you mean to me. You are not just a Scribe partner, you have become a trusted friend and a soul-sister. For ten years I struggled getting words on paper and in six short months, you literally took what was inside my head and helped me create something that I will treasure forever. You are a beautiful gift to this world.

To Captain Florida—thank you from the bottom of my heart for showing me what being rooted in true love can look like. While it is not always easy, it is worth it. Thank you for all of the unsolicited advice that you cannot help but to give. I know you think I don't listen (ever)—I do. Your perspective matters. And thank you for giving new meaning to a simple hyphen.

Finally and most importantly, I want to thank Jesus. When I began writing, I said that I wanted this book to be co-authored and inspired by you. As you always do, you led me exactly where I needed to go. I'm grateful for the soft whispers, the deliberate nudges, and the frying pan moments that helped me grow through change and get rooted in you. May I always be rooted in your principles and do the work that matters most.

ABOUT THE AUTHOR

STACY HENRY is the owner and founder of CenterBranch, a people-centered leadership business dedicated to helping both companies and individuals perform to their highest potential through customized solutions. She is an ICF credentialed executive coach with twenty-five years of global human resources experience. With her impressive credentials and decades of experience, Stacy is often sought out for her expertise in leadership development and change management. Stacy actively coaches several C-Suite leaders in one of the world's largest aerospace and defense companies.

Prior to founding CenterBranch, Stacy held senior leadership roles for a variety of global industries, including Fortune 50 aerospace and defense, Global Fortune 500 automotive, manufacturing, and private equity startups. One of her highest accomplishments, while working corporately, was partnering with Middle Tennessee State University (MTSU) and the

US military academies to develop Tennessee's first stackable undergraduate certificate program in Applied Leadership. This specialized curriculum was designed for the adult learners seeking an undergraduate degree and a leadership role within one of the companies she worked for.

Stacy currently lives in West Palm Beach, Florida, where she enjoys the two seasons—hot and hotter.

To learn more about CenterBranch and how Stacy can enable you or your company to flourish, please visit www. CenterBranch.com or email info@CenterBranch.com

Made in the USA
Middletown, DE
08 January 2021

31115809R00137